From Deep Within
Living Out Of Our Spirit

by John W. Wallace

What People Are Saying About

From Deep Within:

In this book, John opened my spiritual eyes to see the separation of my soul from my spirit—a fact that I had NEVER before been challenged by, which became a truth that has uncaged the Lord's Spirit to give me the rest and power to walk by HIS SPIRIT and not by my soul - fed by my flesh. A CHOICE!

There is a NEW freedom to acknowledge my soul (which was uniquely created by HIM) and choose HIS spiritual food over the world's food to nurture and feed my life. There is the SPIRIT deep within my born again spirit that " is LIFE come daily true " -- always loved and in love!

Like David...I can now turn to my soul and "command" my soul to get rest, strength, hope, lovingkindness, abundance, forgiveness, grace, mercy, truth,...(the list goes on as the hours of the day...) AND to be washed in and fed by HIM --- there (deep within) rather than wallow in the "soul food" of choice, my fears, faults, stress, duty, shame, blame (that list goes on too)

THANK YOU John for revealing HIS promises come true --spirit to SPIRIT, from deep within to overflow out. THIS IS A BOOK THAT BRINGS LIFE TO BE LIVED OUT-- from deep to deep and HIS SPIRIT to spirit.

Debby P.
Interior Designer

I am 64 years old, a committed believer in Jesus my entire life and a very active participant in all kinds Christian activities inside and outside the local church. It has been my blessing to be exposed to many of the best and the brightest Godly leaders and teachers in the Body of Christ. And, it saddens me to admit, that I am a textbook case of someone who has been over-fed and undernourished. With regard to the Holy Spirit and the life of the Spirit I was also woefully underdeveloped. Over the past few years I have sat under John's teaching in a weekly Bible study. God has used John's teaching and personal testimony about the Holy Spirit to literally rock my world. It has been ever so nourishing and practical and liberating and educational!

                                          Jon H.
                                          Discipler & Life Coach

All rights reserved
Copyright: © 2013 John W. Wallace
ISBN: 978-1-940359-01-4
Library of Congress Control Number: 2013949579
Burkhart Books, Bedford, TX 2013

All rights reserved. This book is protected by the copyright laws of the United States of America. This book may not be copied or reprinted for commercial gain or profit. The use of short quotations or occasional page copying for personal group study is permitted and encouraged. Permission will be granted upon request. Unless otherwise identified, scripture quotations are from New American Standard Bible, King James Version, New International Version and New Living Translation. All emphasis within scripture quotations is the author's own.

Burkhart Books

Bedford, TX
www.burkhartbooks.com

TABLE OF CONTENTS

Dedication		7
Forward by Jack R. Taylor		9
Preface		13
Introduction		17
Chapter 1	What Is A Spiritual Person?	23
Chapter 2	Why Is It Important To Be Spiritual?	31
Chapter 3	What is our spirit?	41
Chapter 4	What Does Our Spirit Do?	56
Chapter 5	The Model Spiritual Person	65
Chapter 6	The Holy Spirit In Our Spirit	81
Chapter 7	Living By The Spirit I	120
Chapter 8	Living By The Spirit II	134
An Afterword		157

DEDICATION

I have many mentors in my life. I have been blessed. I guess the Lord knew that I, right from the start of my walk in following Jesus, needed so much help. I have been mentored by so many, through so many means — lectures, books, tapes, videos, DVDs, interviews, mornings or afternoons over coffee and restaurant tables. I have been mentored more by lives than by "steps to spiritual success." An observed life is an advanced education. I dedicate these words I've written to all those who have invested in my life and ministry, those aware and unaware. Some include Sam Owen, Steve Atkinson, Don Sunujikan, Walter Bodine, John Wimber, David Van Cronkhite, Mike Bickle, Ben Fike, and my spiritual "Papa" Jack Taylor.

Perhaps the most profound mentor I've experienced is my wife Suzanne. Her persistent passion to live deeply and productively for her God and Father has provoked, shamed, lured, excited, and led me to breathe more deeply of the atmosphere of the Spirit and enjoy the ambiance of heaven. Not only do I dedicate this work to you, but, as I believe you know, I am dedicated to you!

I join the Apostle Paul in proclaiming, "By the grace of God, I am what I am" (1 Corinthians 15:10). I am a graced man!

FOREWORD

I have written more than a few endorsements, forwards, forewords, introductions, prefaces and the like. I invariably love the experience. My habit generally begins with meditation on the kind of man (or woman) the author is. The better I know him (or her) the more joyous the experience. The better I know the author the easier the task. I was, at first in this business (recommending books) rather ill at ease, because the time frame was always against the possibility of reading the book as thoroughly as it deserved and I desired. Deadlines notwithstanding, I have at times only made a rapid journey through the manuscript, seeking to get a sense of direction and destination added to constant prayer for anointing to do the book justice. This experience has been a memorable one among the memorables!

With this book let me begin by saying that I am wildly in love with the title as well as the subtitle. Captured in the title is an ocean of needed and presented truth, "From Deep Within". The subtitle, "Living Out of Our Spirit" is as freighted with intrigue and potential as the title, "From Deep Within". My early response was, "Wish I had thought of that!"

This is a book not only about the Holy Spirit, but a revelation about the human spirit. If the Holy Spirit is the Star and He is, the human spirit is the supporting cast. Revelation about the former will mean clearer revelation about the latter. As these two subjects are approached together as the central cast, the human soul explodes with good sense and overflowing revelation, supplying a perfect "supporting cast".

There is no way this subject matter can serve to fill the role of a satisfying totality in this one book, but the manner in which this brilliant former Doctor of Dentistry seems to navigate the massive ocean of truth with enormous ease and accuracy, sequence and timing, makes it seem "the final word". The wording is precise, clear and loudly invites pursuit. The movement is thorough enough to capture the fancy of the reader, leaving a voracious appetite for the much more that is expected just around the corner or down the road. Pregnant phrases and word pictures, coupled with the strange experience of identifying with the author in the "before", the "after" and "the later after-whiles," all gravitate toward one crescendo after another. Installed near my heart is a pacer/defibrillator, my second one. (The first one saved my life, but almost killed me in the process!) The second one with an extra lead directly into the heart was installed after a double heart attack. In the midst of the journey through this book I actually experienced a momentary fear that the "defib" would fire because of the elevated number of beats in my heart. Thank God it didn't and as I thought about it later (the rapid beating), though it was elevated, it remained ordered and properly paced. I anticipate that the readers of this volume will experience something akin to this and, with me, will need to recalibrate the excitement at the prospects of living from within with His Spirit in ours; the way we were made to live.

From origination to destination we, the readers, will travel a thrilling and radiant landscape dotted with colorful tales that derive from living out of our spirits. I confidently suggest that you will find great pleasure in the journey mapped in this brilliant work, revel in the fact that this journey has only begun, and celebrate the fact that the trip is not only cosmic, thus all inclusive, but eternal, therefore never ending!

A word to wise seems sufficient: After you have finished these pages, pick up John's first book, *Kingdom Come! Tales of the Supernatural God,* keep them close together for later

Kingdom learning and revelation. Enjoy the experience to the depths where His Spirit resides in yours and opens a flowing fountain that never ceases. I have some books that I keep with me most everywhere I go. They are of the kind that you can open at virtually any page and find the flow within.

To the author, "Thanks, John!" and to the reader, "Bon voyage!"

Jack R. Taylor, President
Dimensions Ministries
Melbourne, Florida

PREFACE

I have lived most of my life out of my soul. I have thought my way through life or relied upon my feelings or a combination of the two and have made decisions, some very crucial decisions, on the basis of these "soulish" directives.

When I accepted Jesus over 40 years ago, I saw only sporadic change in the way my life was being directed. I still relied upon how I thought about things: adding to my intellectual pursuit of secular knowledge an intellectual pursuit of spiritual knowledge. I was led to believe that the more I knew, the better I'd be. I also relied upon how I felt about things, somehow hoping or trusting that now my emotions were under the control of the Holy Spirit. And the choices I made relied upon the other two, my intellect and my feelings. I knew that God's Holy Spirit lived in me —somewhere. I asked His guidance. I asked Him to bless what I was thinking and feeling and choosing.

It wasn't until several years ago that I began to study, meditate upon, and work out my, now firmly-held, conviction that we believers in Christ are, in the deepest essence of our beings, spiritual. This conviction isn't theoretical or theological. This is an experienced conviction! We have access to spiritual realities that few of us tap into. Our spirits are crucial parts of us that are "really alive."

That's what this book is about: tapping into a spiritual life that, I believe, our heavenly Father has made available to us. Because I am a lover of God's word, the Bible, and a student of it, there's a lot of Scripture within these pages. But that's just to demonstrate God's passion, communicated to us for our greatest welfare: that we might live closely related to Him and fully out of our spirit.

We will entertain the question "What is a spiritual person?" We will look at what our spirit is and how it was designed to function. Then we will ask a question that has become standard for me: "What does it look like?" I'm not seeking knowledge, as good as it may be, unless it is "applicable knowledge." I want to see how it works.

Finally, I'll share with you some tips or suggestions for Living Deeply, living out of your spirit. I share these tips with some caution. I've found that we can rarely, if ever, deepen our spiritual lives by methods or steps. The "activities" that I share with you have helped me. But I'm far, far from being a person who constantly and consistently lives out of his spirit. I'm still learning from our Lord and from His people. I see it as a journey. I'm on it. I'm some ways down the highway, maybe a little further than you or trying to catch up to you. But I'm on it. I have now, as one of my highest priorities, to live out of my spirit. I believe that's what we were made for.

You might be asking, "Who is this guy?" Well, many people want a label. I mean, we want to identify people according to which Christian camp they are a part of. So, let me give you some labels. First, from one point of view, I'm a Christian "continuationist." What I mean by "continuationist" is that I believe we are to continue to believe the Scriptural promises our God has given us. I believe we are to continue to come to God through faith in His Son Jesus and Jesus' redemptive work on the cross and resurrection. I believe we are to continue to believe that God's word is living and active. I believe we are to continue to believe that Jesus left us here on earth to be the physical and spiritual representation of His body. I believe that we are to continue to operate in all of the gifts of the Spirit. I believe we are to continue to believe and carry out His great commission to disciple the nations.

Next, from another point of view, I'm an "Evangelical." I was brought to Christ through an evangelical, para-church organization. I was "raised" in the faith by several evangelical teachers and pastors. I received theological education from several evangelical schools and graduated from an evangelical seminary. However, when some evangelicals look at some of what I believe and some of what I practice they would label me a charismatic Christian. They say, since I believe in the practice of all of the gifts of the Spirit and because I encourage healing ministry, I'm a charismatic (however, many charismatics would say I'm not a REAL, full-blown charismatic). Now, let me give you my label for myself. I'm an evangematic. I try to draw from the greatest and deepest truths, as I understand them, from the "best" of the Evangelical world and the "best" from the Charismatic world. So, if you're looking for a label, something to identify me with, theologically, that's it.

Actually, I'm just a follower of Christ who, for the past 28 years, has tried to be faithful in the ministry of pastoring the dear folks our Father has privileged me to serve. As I said, I'm on a journey ... a journey to explore the depths of God. So, let's explore together how to LIVE DEEPLY.

JohnW. Wallace
December 2012

INTRODUCTION

"I wanted to live deep and suck out all the marrow of life...and not, when I came to die, discover I had not lived."
–Henry David Thoreau

"I know following Jesus ought to be more 'exciting,' but it just seems boring, a drudgery."

"There's got to be more than I'm experiencing."

"Life is really hard. I seem to be, you know, 'tossed about by every wave.'"

"I'm realizing that much of the time I'm motivated by a bunch of feelings: anger, depression, doubt, shame, and fear. What do I do?"

"I know, intellectually, that God is here. I know, intellectually, that He loves me. I know that my faith should be a relationship with Him. But that's not been my track record. I sure don't sense that."

"I'm a Christian. But I don't see God at work in my life."

"There has to be more."

If any of these conversations have been made or thought by you, then I believe I have some encouragement and suggestions for you. Life in Christ IS supposed to be more—more than intellectual and more than getting jerked around by our emotions. Life with Father (Jesus said He wants to bring us to a Father) IS supposed to be abundant, filled with joy, overcoming doubt, guilt, anger, and a host of other dynamics that regularly rob us and sap our energy, time, and attention. If you are feeling or thinking any of this, READ ON. We weren't created to be "natural" people but "spiritual" people. Father speaks to that in 1 Corinthians 2 (see the next chapter). I believe what follows will help you get there.

Have you ever had the same thought as Thoreau? Have you wondered if you are living life "deeply"? Jesus Christ said, "I came that they may have life and have it abundantly" (John 10:10). Is there a part of us, deep, deep within, from which this abundant life may be lived? I'm talking about ABUNDANT life. Are we really meant to be deeply spiritual beings living life from deep within? Who is "spiritual"? What does a "spiritual" person look like? Is it really important to be spiritual? Can being spiritual be separated from other aspects of living? These questions and similar ones are what have generated this book.

I have walked through this journey of life for over six decades. In the course of traveling it I have found that I have not lived life as "deeply" as I may have desired. I have not, to use Thoreau's words, sucked "out all the marrow of life." A few years back I began to question why this has been true. Why have the distractions and the urgencies of day-to-day existence robbed me of some deeper, more abundant living? As a follower of Jesus, I had to look afresh at how He, and His word, spoke of life. I had to re-examine who I was and the purposes for which I had been created. I had to assess if I was living a truly "spiritual life." Now, I'm not talking about a religious life. We'll talk about that later. Religious and spiritual are two entirely different things. Religion can pose as spirituality, but that isn't living as we were meant to live. Jesus confronted those, in His days on earth, who were posers — substituting religious beliefs and practices as spiritual.

Therefore I went on an expedition. Or, perhaps, a better

word would be a re-tracing of my steps back to see where I strayed from this path of deep living. I analyzed how I have been living life and what has robbed me of abundant living. Then I asked how I could access the deepest part of me from which, I have become convinced, I must live life.

I've presented this material by way of talks to groups of Christians. So often the ensuing discussions from such feedback sounds like this: "You're right, I've lived this soulish way myself" or "This spiritual life is what my wife and I have been talking about!" or "We Christians need to be challenged to live this way." The ensuing discussions from such questions have been stimulating and, I trust, life-giving to those in the groups I've addressed. I've tried to interject some of those questions along the way. I hope they are some of the same ones you might ask if we were having a conversation about life.

Now, I'm not a "word-y" person. I don't elaborate much. I try to write the same way I talk. I get to the point, trying to illustrate it in Scripture and then from current experience. Then I look at how I can put these truths and spiritual dynamics into practice. Therefore, this isn't a long book. It's short. This is for several reasons. First, I believe we are living in a culture that, by and large, isn't much of a reading culture anymore. In our culture people, especially young people, like their information brief, "bite" size. They won't go research Encyclopedia Britannica but they might check out Wikipedia online. Short updates on Facebook or short Youtube segments are what they go for. A bunch of words on a page won't hold their attention very long. Second, I honestly don't want to spend a huge amount of time writing on this topic. Why? Because I want to get it out in circulation quickly. Besides, the Apostle Paul said that "the kingdom of God does not consist of words but of power" (1 Cor. 4:20). So,

I'm more for challenging you to live this out—powerfully—than I am to write and write and write about it. I'm convinced we live in an era that will quickly divide real Christians from those who only say they are. I believe it will be more and more important to live life spiritually as followers of Jesus. I believe a life of contrast, a light in the midst of darkness, will soon be more evident than it ever has before.

And so, I present this to you for your consideration, prayer, and interaction. Whatever your response, I do challenge you to learn to live deeply. If you have met the Lord Jesus Christ, you have His Holy Spirit living in the deepest part of you, in your spirit. Get in touch with Him and live from there. If you haven't exchanged your life for Jesus' life, I urge you (especially after reading this) to do so.

Chapter One

WHAT IS A SPIRITUAL PERSON?

1 Cor. 2:14 But a natural man does not accept the things of the Spirit of God, for they are foolishness to him; and he cannot understand them, because they are spiritually appraised. 15 But he who is spiritual appraises all things, yet he himself is appraised by no one.

Recently I took a round-trip plane ride to Kansas City. I had to get up very early to get to the airport. Sitting at the gate waiting to board the aircraft I was looking forward to just relaxing or getting a short nap on the way up. No sooner had I thought of this, that another thought – stronger and deeper – penetrated me: the Lord wants me to minister to someone on the plane. "OK, OK, Lord." Once onboard, I was seated next to a young woman who, I could see, was part of a youth group or college group traveling to KC. On the way, the Lord began to "download" information about this woman's life to me. This isn't an unusual occurrence in my life. It is, I'm convinced, a spiritual gift that operates within me. Later in the flight I turned to her and said, "Excuse me, I know this sounds weird. But if what I'm about to say means anything to you, please think about it. If it doesn't, just throw it in the trash and consider that you just met a weird old man on the plane." I proceeded to tell her the information the Lord had given me for her. I told her I believed that I received this from God. As I talked, she began to tear up. I can usually tell if the "knowledge" the Lord has given me is accurate or not. This was. At the end, I told her that this God loved her so much that He would tell a stranger this info to let her know how much He loved her and wanted her to know Him and His son. He wanted her to know and believe how crazing-in-love He was with her.

At the same exact time, my wife Suzanne was driving on the interstate in the driving rain back in Dallas. As she exited on the off-ramp, she first noticed a disabled vehicle on the ramp and then, a few yards ahead, a woman walking up the ramp in this downpour. Almost all of the time Suzanne DOES NOT pick people up. But something, deep inside, let her know that she needed to stop. Her stopping started a 3 hour chain-of-events that left this woman also believing in the God who loved her.

Both of these events illustrate a sensitivity to living out of our spirit. I sensed that our Father wanted to communicate to the young woman on the plane. My wife sensed that our Father wanted to demonstrate His love to the woman in the rain.

So let's look at what Father has to say in His Word, the Bible.

Bible translation is an interesting process. The translator must know the original languages, the grammar, the variant readings of the early manuscripts, and have some handle on the individual words and their meanings, both in their "secular" usage as well as their use and any variation in the Scriptures. Then he or she (the translator) must try to bring that meaning, as closely as possible, into our language for our understanding.

In our 1 Corinthian passage above we've been served a disservice, I believe. I've checked many English translations of these verses. The words "natural man" occur in most of them. A few translations say "the man without the Spirit" (NIV) or "the unspiritual" (New Revised Standard). But the word translated "natural" (NASB), is the Greek word *psuchikos*. It means "soulish." We get our English word "psychology" from it.

Paul is rebuking the Corinthians for living out of their souls and not out of their spirits. The contrast he emphasizes is between a life lived that is "soulish" and a life lived that is "spiritual." When we (even us Christians) live out of our soul, (when our soul in control), when we are "soulish," In that case, Paul says (3:1), we are "men of flesh." We are "infants" (Greek *nephios* = simple-minded, immature, baby-ish). We haven't grown up at all.

I've read and read and re-read this passage in the Greek language and in many, many English translations. I've meditated upon these words of God to me ... to us. I want to be a spiritual man. I want to live "out of" my spirit, not out of my soul. And because I love my Father so much, because I want to live a life that pleases and honors Him, and partner with His Spirit in impacting the world around me, I know I can do that by growing up. If you've read this far, then you, too, have a desire to be a spiritual person and live deeply and grow up.

What does it mean to be "spiritual"? What is a "spiritual" person? Apparently, as we see from these scriptures, being a spiritual person is very, very important. Is being spiritual the same thing as knowing a lot of the Bible or keeping our emotions "under control"? I think not.

As I've written in my preface and introduction, it's my conviction that we, including myself, have lived most of our Christian life out of our soul and not out of our spirit. I think that we think and feel and choose our way through life. That is what I would call living out of the soul. Most scholarship says, in the secular as well as the spiritual circles, that the soul is composed of our mind, our will, and our emotions — so our thinker, our feeler and our chooser. So most of us live our lives out of one of those or a combination of two or three of those.

What's the difference between living a soulish life and living a spiritual life?

Could we say that soulish living is sensory living? We've been created with five natural senses: sight, hearing, smell, taste and touch. We experience life through these senses. How we perceive and respond to these experiences is, most often, processed in our soul. Soulish living is limited to our experiences or the experiences of others, whereas spiritual living transitions out of these dimensions and into God's dimensions so that now God chooses what we think and feel and choose. Our spirit becomes our "processor" and "command center" for living.

Our soul isn't bad. Our soul isn't wrong. We are created with a mind. We are made with emotions. Since we are made in the image of God, we have a will as He does. We are to worship the Father with all parts of our being: "And He [Jesus] said to him, 'YOU SHALL LOVE THE LORD YOUR GOD WITH ALL YOUR HEART, AND WITH ALL YOUR SOUL, AND WITH ALL YOUR MIND'" (Matthew 22:37). The issue at hand isn't whether the soul is good. The issue at hand is whether the soul is good enough to make us "spiritual." The issue is what will govern us. Will our mind, our emotions, and our will govern us or will God govern us from our spirit?
God desires to captivate our soul, that is, to bring it under control. We are going to see that David steps outside of himself and commands his soul to get in line. Psalm 103:1-2: "Bless the Lord, O my soul...."

So, again, "What is a spiritual person?" We have answers both from the world and from the church:

The world, of course, has a multitude of experts to give answers to our question. "Who is spiritual" gets responses from the Dahli Lama (or some other religious leader) to poets, artists, and philosophers. What does, then, a spiritual person look like to them? A person who does good, is charitable, cares for the "downtrodden", looks at the world "wholistically", is very tolerant, is considered spiritual. Consider this interchange between Oprah Winfrey and members of her television studio audience (2008):

Oprah: One of the mistakes that human beings make is believing that there is only one way to live and that we don't accept that there are diverse ways of being in the world, that there are millions of ways to please God and many ways, many paths to what you call God.

Audience member 1: And I guess the danger that could be in …I mean it sounds great at the onset but if you really look at both sides…

Oprah: There couldn't possibly be just one way!

Audience member 2: You say there isn't only one way. There is one way and only one way and that is through Jesus.

Oprah: There couldn't possibly be only one way with millions of people in the world!

Or, take Julia Roberts spirituality:

Clarifying that actual spiritual satisfaction was the real reason behind her converting to Hinduism, Julia Roberts said, "I have no intention of demeaning any other religion simply because of my fondness for Hinduism. I don't believe in comparing religions or human beings. A comparison is a very mean thing to do. I have received real spiritual satisfaction through Hinduism."

The Dahli Lama is guided by three major commitments: the promotion of basic human values or secular ethics in the interest of human happiness, the fostering of inter-religious harmony and the welfare of the Tibetan people. [from www.dahlilama.com]

["Secular ethics" – what's that? Ethics are the moral values, the accepted 'rules of conduct' of right and wrong within a culture. By using the term "secular" the Lama has taken right and wrong out of the arena of God and placed it into the arena of human beings.]

"Human happiness" – this, apparently, is one of the highest goals of the Lama. Happiness, however, is relative to what I determine makes me happy. God's goal is our holiness, which He says will give us ultimate satisfaction: "In Your presence is the fullness of joy" (Psalm 16:11).]

New Age spirituality has been described as "drawing both on Eastern and Western spiritual and metaphysical traditions and infusing them with influences from self-help and motivational psychology, holistic health, parapsychology, consciousness research, and quantum physics."

Also, included as "spiritual people" in the world's view are artists and poets. A spiritual person might be seen as one who, true to New Age philosophy, is "at one with the universe." And there are many ways offered to make you a "spiritual" person — from reading poetry to meditating to smoking weed. So, maybe you've not bought into the world's definition of who is spiritual, but you've bought into the church's.

The church has its own definition of who is spiritual. A spiritual person is one who prays all the time or knows the Bible (can quote it, has large portions memorized) or a person who regularly tithes their money. A spiritual person might be one who doesn't get mad ("Oh, they are really NICE.") or who remains sexually pure. The list or the criteria may include any number of things depending upon what is important in that particular culture or church. I know of one church culture where a man isn't spiritual unless he wears a tie to church!

Is there any standard for spirituality? Yes. May I give you my definition of a spiritual person? *A spiritual person is a person who is living, at any given moment, out of their spirit.* A spiritual Christian person is a person who lives out of their spirit, which is inhabited, controlled, filled, empowered and informed by God's Holy Spirit. Paul says "he who is spiritual appraises all things." That is, a truly spiritual person is able to evaluate all things in his/her life from a spiritual point-of-view.

Using this definition, I want to explore what it means to be a spiritual person. I want to discuss why I feel it is so important to be truly spiritual as we seek to be influencers of the kingdom of God in this world. I'm challenging all of us to begin to live out of our spirits instead of out of alternatives we have chosen ... more on that in Chapter 3.

SUMMARY

- The contrast in 1 Corinthians 2 is "soulish" living vs. "spiritual" living.
- Our soul is good; it just isn't supposed to be in control.
- Our soul is our thinker (mind), feeler (emotions), and chooser (will).
- A spiritual person is one who is living out of their spirit.

Questions

1. What composes our soul?
2. Have I spent a good deal of my life living out of my soul?
3. What is the definition given of a "spiritual" person?
4. Does this definition seem right to me?
5. Do I have a hunger to be a truly, spiritual person?

Chapter 2

WHY IS IT IMPORTANT TO BE SPIRITUAL?

Gal. 6:1 Brethren, even if anyone is caught in any trespass, you who are spiritual, restore such a one in a spirit of gentleness; each one looking to yourself, so that you too will not be tempted.

A number of years ago, our friends, Ted and Michala, moved to Jersusalem to join a prayer ministry there. This was during the time when several terrorist bombs were going off in the city. This dear couple needed to go each day to the market (they didn't have a refrigerator in their apartment). So, each time they left their apartment building they had to ask the Lord which way to walk. Some days they received a strong impression to walk to the left, some of the days they received just such an impression to walk to the right. Their lives and safety depended daily on their ability to receive and follow direction from the Lord. Although our physical lives may not depend on our ability to be spiritual, like Ted and Michala, our spiritual lives do.

The above passage from Galatians calls upon those who are "spiritual" to restore a person caught in a trespass. Sounds like it was/is important to be able to determine who is spiritual and who isn't, doesn't it? Looking in the Bible, why is it important or how important is it, to be spiritual or to be able to determine if you are spiritual?

First, being spiritual is like having the right "radar." It connects me to something way beyond myself. It connects us with the greater reality. It's a matter of which reality you want to live in. Jesus, standing before Pilate before His scourging and crucifixion, gave an answer to Pilate's question about

His kingship. "Jesus answered, 'My kingdom is not of this world. If My kingdom were of this world, then My servants would be fighting so that I would not be handed over to the Jews; but as it is, My kingdom is not of this realm'" (John 18:36). Jesus' kingdom was "not of this realm." His kingdom is not, literally (Greek) "from here" or "from this side." His kingdom emanated from another realm, another "side." Yet, He began His earthly ministry by saying that kingdom had arrived; it was "at hand" (Mark 1:14-15). That's the realm I want to live "out of" – the kingdom-of-God realm. That kingdom is the greater reality. That kingdom reality must govern all that I encounter in this "earthly" reality.

We can think that way, we can desire that way, but we don't usually live that way. When push comes to shove, amidst daily circumstances, how we react to those circumstances, (the majority of the time) has been in a soulish way instead of a spiritual way. I've lived more out of this reality instead of the kingdom reality. For example, when you get under a lot of pressure to come up with an answer to a problem, do you spend a lot of time thinking about it? Do you worry about it? Do you have a hard time, especially if people are involved, because your emotions play a great part?

Most people don't know what you are talking about when you mention true spiritual living. We've read these passages about spiritual living, and we have not recognized the gap between how we live life and how our Father's Word describes it. Or maybe we have seen the difference but don't know how to move into true, spiritual living.

Over the years we've heard sermons about the spiritual life. We've read books about the spiritual life. Those messages and words usually center around DOING spiritual disciplines. In other words, how we become spiritual is by having more devotional times, memorizing the Bible, praying more, giving more, and harnessing our sin (attitudes and actions). I'm not suggesting we stop these disciplines. But they, in themselves, are no guarantee of spirituality. It's a radical thought that a spiritual person is a SPIRITUAL person!

A friend of mine has a Christian friend who is going through a divorce. The man has 5 prayers (printed out) that he prays every day. My friend said to him, "Don't you ever want to just tell God what's on your heart?" Good question! What's the difference between reading the 5 prayers over and over and talking to God? It sounds like the man is using printed prayers like some kind of tool to manipulate events. Perhaps I'm unfairly evaluating the situation. Perhaps this man genuinely enters into the prayers and they are meaningful and transforming to him. It's just that the report given to me was that this man felt that if he prayed these prayers enough, things would change. The prayers were tools to leverage the situation. We can get to the point where we have more faith in the tool than in the One with Whom nothing is too difficult (Jeremiah 32:27).

The **second reason** being spiritual is important is because God says He wants to connect with us in our "spirit." Jesus says, in John 17:3 "This is eternal life, that they may know You, the only true God, and Jesus Christ whom You have sent." Eternal life is personal (not intellectual) knowledge of the Father and the Son. The apostle John reinforces this truth: "What was from the beginning, what we have heard, what we have seen with our eyes, what we have looked at and touched with our hands, concerning the Word of Life — and the life was manifested, and we have seen and testify and proclaim to you the eternal life, which was with the Father and was manifested to us — what we have seen and heard we proclaim to you also, so that you too may have fellowship with us; and indeed our fellowship is with the Father, and with His Son Jesus Christ" (1 John 1:1-3). In other words, John is saying, "We've experienced eternal life. This life I'm talking about requires fellowship, a relationship." John uses words like "we heard' and "seen with our eyes" and "looked at" and "touched". We Christians say that our faith is about a relationship. But for many of us, at the beginning of our spiritual walk we say a prayer (the prayer of salvation), come into that relationship, and immediately start keeping rules, because rules are measureable. Rules help us know how we are doing. And they soothe our conscience when we compare ourselves to others. "I know I'm not praying enough but I know I pray more than James (or Betty or whomever). But how can you measure a relationship? It is measurable, but usually not day-to-day or with a checklist. How would that work with our relationships with our spouse, our family, our close friends? "Honey, let me see how our relationship is going. I'll just pull out my checklist."

A spiritual relationship IS measurable. A "measure" of that relationship is the presence or quality of intimacy with Him. How well do I know God ... not "know about" God but really KNOW God? How much time, uninterrupted and focused, do I spend with Him? Do we have dialogue? Every good relationship has two-way communication. How often do I sense His presence with me? Also measurable is the evidence of fruit of the spirit. Fruit is a measurement of that relationship. A degree of intimacy is the measure of that relationship. If the presence of God is living in me by the Holy Spirit, then I will see evidence: love, joy, peace, patience, kindness, goodness, faith, gentleness, and self control (Galatians 5:22-23).

What about my times of worship? Jesus told the woman at the well that God is spirit. Those that worship Him must worship in spirit and truth. Many times we will say we had a great worship experience. Is it more likely that we just had our emotions stirred? Or did we encounter the living God and acknowledge His infinite value (the meaning of worship)? Granted, we can worship both in soul and spirit. But just an emotional worship is only part of the picture. We must worship Him in spirit.

Third, in a verse earlier in the 1 Cor. 2 passage, it says "THINGS WHICH EYE HAS NOT SEEN AND EAR HAS NOT HEARD, AND which HAVE NOT ENTERED THE HEART OF MAN, ALL THAT GOD HAS PREPARED FOR THOSE WHO LOVE HIM" (v. 9). It's important that we be spiritual people because it is in our spirit that God shows us things we haven't experienced in the natural realm. God has prepared for us who love Him things that haven't even entered the heart of man, things which we haven't seen or heard. We talked earlier about our soul basing its reality on the things we and others have experienced. But God's reality includes things "out there" for us that we haven't experienced. Paul continues in Corinthians, "For God has revealed them through the Spirit ... so that we may know the things freely given to us by God." In the spirit, in the spirit, these spiritual realities are revealed through the Spirit in our spirit.

Fourth, in our spirit is where inner strength lies. "For this reason I bow my knees before the Father, from whom every family in heaven and on earth derives its name, that He would grant you, according to the riches of His glory, to be strengthened with power through His Spirit in the inner man, so that Christ may dwell in your hearts through faith; and that you, being rooted and grounded in love, may be able to comprehend with all the saints what is the breadth and length and height and depth, and to know the love of Christ which surpasses knowledge, that you may be filled up to all the fullness of God" (Eph. 3:14-19). Paul's prayer for the Ephesians (and us) is that, ultimately, we would be filled up. What a prayer: to be filled to the fullness of God!! But where does that prayer begin? It begins with the prayer for strength/power through the Holy Spirit. Where? In our inner man = our spirit.

Incidentally, most people would to say the dimensions (height and depth and length and breadth, v. 18) refer to love. Some English translations convey that (NIV, NLT, The Message). But grammatically that's not true. The verses say "may be able to comprehend with all the saints what is the breadth and length and height and depth, AND to know the love of Christ which surpasses knowledge, that you may be filled up to all the fullness of God." If I said, "bread and butter" is the bread butter or the butter bread? No. They are two separate objects joined by the conjunction "and." Paul wants the Ephesians (and us) to know the dimensions of something (unnamed) and he wants us to know the love of Christ. What do the dimensions refer to?

Of all Paul's epistles, Ephesians has the most to say about spiritual warfare and the demonic realm. Remember in Acts 19 when Paul ministered in Ephesus, people were being converted and brought their magic books to burn in the fire? Why? Ephesus was the center of black magic. From ancient magical documents of the time, the dark powers were called "the height and depth and length and breadth" (check out "Power and Magic: The Concept of Power in Ephesians" by Clinton Arnold). Paul is praying that we would know REAL power (to overcome spiritual darkness) and REAL love.

Where did this prayer start? "Strengthened with power in the inner man." Where did this prayer end? "filled up with all the fullness of God." That's how important it is to be spiritual!

To be spiritual is to live with this kind of wonderful power that leads to being full of God.

Also we are to wage war in the spirit (Eph. 6:10ff.). We don't wrestle with flesh and blood but with spiritual powers. And in 2 Cor. 10 we don't wage this war with fleshly weapons. It's important to be spiritual so that we can be victorious in spiritual battle. Most of us wage spiritual war with intellectual weapons.

Fifth, in Rom. 8:13 Paul says something similar: *"for if you are living according to the flesh, you must die; but if by the Spirit you are putting to death the deeds of the body, you will live."* How do you put to death the misdeeds of the body? By the Spirit. Where does His Holy Spirit dwell? In our spirit. You don't put to death the misdeeds of the body by discipline. You don't put them to death by will power. You don't put them to death by right thinking. Those may come into play. But where you start is "by the spirit." You can't fight the flesh with the soul. You fight the flesh with the spirit. That's the only way to have victory over the flesh: by the spirit. If we do try to kill the flesh with soulish power, especially if it looks like we are doing well, it feeds our ego, our pride (because WE were able to do this).

My goal is to get people to stay in this growth process, or better, to GET into the process. I've found many Christians aren't even aware of their spirit. The growth process takes place more supernaturally natural if our spiritual nature is emphasized early on instead of having to learn or un-learn many things later.

Recently, my wife and I returned from the Leadership Advance Conference in Redding, California. While there we were given the opportunity to have a 3-person "prophetic team" to minister us, praying and prophesying over us. Each team had a child on it. A child. A child, nurtured in this kind of environment stressing spiritual growth, can hear the voice of the Lord and communicate it. Our team, prophesying and praying over my wife and I, had a 12 year old girl. Her "words" and encouragements were the most accurate of any other team member.

Sixth, Gal. 5:25-26 says: *"If we live by the Spirit let us walk by the Spirit."*

"Walk" means "keep in step" and "follow". It's a military term (marching rank and file). When you are marching, you keep in step with the person in front of you. If you are going to live by the Spirit, stay in step with the Spirit; if He moves His right foot, you move your right foot. If He moves His left foot, you move that one. If He does "column left" or "column right" you do too. Don't keep going straight if He turns! Walking by the Spirit means step by step, keep Him in your sights, That necessitates that we keep close to the Spirit. If I don't keep close and I'm ½ block away and He gets to the corner and turns, when I eventually get there, I'm wondering which way He went. Where did He go? This "walking" necessitates us keeping close to the Spirit. That what our friends in Jerusalem had to do every day!

Seventh, consider 1 Thess. 5:23: *Now may the God of peace Himself sanctify you entirely; and may your spirit and soul and body be preserved complete, without blame at the coming of our Lord Jesus Christ.*

Paul speaks here of spirit, soul, body. All three are to be sanctified (set apart to God, set apart as holy) entirely, kept blameless; all three are to be kept blameless. What does the Christian community focus on to be kept blameless?

First the body — don't have sex, don't take drugs, etc.—the don'ts. Some go to the soul. But how do you keep your soul blameless? Similarly, 2 Cor. 7:1 — *"cleansed from everything that defiles flesh and spirit"* — what does that mean? Can our spirit be "defiled?" Absolutely. It can be defiled. Our spirit needs to be kept blameless. It can be slimed, corrupted, dirtied: therefore, the apostolic prayer for its sanctification.

Eighth, it's important for us to be spiritual in order to minister to others. It's important because that's the way Jesus ministered: *"I only do what I see the Father doing"* (John 5:19). In Luke 4 (verse 18) He says that the Spirit of the Lord has *"anointed"* Him to do this ministry. He told the Pharisees, *"But if I, by the Spirit of God, cast out demons, then the kingdom of God has come upon you"* (Matthew 12:28). So, ministry must take place out of our spirit, the Holy Spirit in our spirit. That's what happened to my wife and I in the separate incidents I reported at the beginning of chapter 1. Therefore, for these reasons, and many more, it is important to be a spiritual person. We will continue our journey to becoming more spiritual in Chapter 3.

SUMMARY

- Being spiritual connects me with "radar" (seeing the spiritual world).
- Being spiritual connects me with God.
- Being spiritual connects me with things I haven't experienced.
- Being spiritual connects me with an "inner" strength.
- Being spiritual puts to death the flesh.
- Being spiritual keeps me in step with the Spirit of God.
- Being spiritual helps me minister to others.

Questions

1. How is being spiritual like having spiritual "radar"?
2. How "personal" is my relationship with the Father and the Son?
3. Do I worship the Lord "in spirit and in truth"?
4. Have you ever received something from the Lord that "eye has not seen and ear has not heard"?
5. Would you say that you are strong in your "inner man"?
6. Do you engage in spiritual warfare with spiritual weapons?

Chapter 3

WHAT IS OUR SPIRIT?

Have you ever just "known" something? I mean that, all of sudden, you just knew that you knew something about a person or situation. It wasn't something you thought of. It wasn't something you observed. I wasn't something you felt. You just knew. I offer to you that the "knowing" you experienced probably came out of your spirit.

What we see is that the word "spirit" (Hebrew, *ruach*) isn't used very often in the Old Testament to refer to the human spirit. Occasionally you see it. Most of the time, "spirit" refers to the Spirit of God, the Holy Spirit. When referring to the inner part of man, the Old Testament more often refers to man's "soul". However, when we arrive in the New Testament the term "soul" diminishes greatly in its usage and the term "spirit" skyrockets. Why? We will see the answer as we look at the various Scriptural terms for our human makeup. God has made us "fearfully and wonderfully" (Psalm 139:14), a complexity of various parts. So, in our quest to become more acquainted with our spirit, we will look at these various parts of our nature that the Word speaks of.

The word of God tells us that there is a material and an immaterial part of us. It calls the material part the "outer man" and the immaterial part the "inner man":

> 2 Cor. 4:16 *Therefore we do not lose heart, but though our* **outer man** *is decaying, yet our* **inner man** *is being renewed day by day"* — my wife's favorite birthday verse!

> Romans 7: 22-23 *"For I joyfully concur with the law of God in the inner man, but I see a different law in the members of my body, waging war against the law of my mind and making me a prisoner of the law of sin which is in my members."*

Paul's struggle in Romans 7 is that the inner part of his nature wants to do God's will but his outer man doesn't. Who is going to save him (at the end of chapter 7)? He gives the answer is Romans 8 — living by the spirit/Spirit.

Let's look at the different biblical terms for what we are talking about.

OUR SPIRIT

In Hebrew the word is *ruach* = *receive*; in the Greek language the word is *pneuma*. In both languages the word means wind, spirit, and/or breath. So in 2 Tim. 3:16 when it says that all Scripture is *"inspired by God"* the word is *theo-pneustos* = God breathed. In John 21 where it says, "Jesus said, 'Receive the Holy Spirit.' And He breathed on them" it is a play on words = received the Holy Spirit (pneuma, breath) and He breathed on them.

Look at several passages that emphasize this inner part of us, the spirit:

> Genesis 41:8 – Pharaoh (not a believer) *"now in the morning his spirit was troubled."*

> Psalm 51:10 – at the end of David's great confession of sin, *"and renew a steadfast spirit"* (a strong, stable and persevering spirit); David recognized his spirit.

Therefore our spirit was created to be a container. It is like the ark of the Covenant which "contained" the presence of God.

> Rom. 1:9 – Paul says, *"for God Whom I serve in my spirit"* (at least one English version translates this as "I serve with my whole heart"; there is a fine distinction between heart and spirit as we shall see later).

> 1 Cor. 14:14-15 – *"if I pray in a tongue my spirit prays but my mind is unfruitful"* (Paul distinguishes between his spirit and his mind). "What is the outcome then? I will pray with the spirit and I will pray with the mind also; I will sing with the spirit and I will sing with the mind also." When I was in seminary, our professor told us that the "spirit" here meant emotions. It was, he interpreted, the difference between worshipping God emotionally or intellectually! Really?

We do see here the recognition and operation of the spirit of man in both non-believers and believers.

OUR SOUL

In Hebrew, the word is *nephesh*; in the Greek the word is psyche (from which we get the word psychology). Interestingly, in Genesis 2:7 it says "Then the LORD God formed man of dust from the ground, and breathed into his nostrils the breath of life; and man became a living being" (NASB). In the Hebrew it says "and man became a living soul (*nephesh*)." Adam's soul came alive when God breathed into him.

Now, once I had done a comparative study of "spirit" and "soul" from Genesis to Revelation, I realized that the emphasis on the nature of man in the Old Testament is on the "soul." The emphasis on the nature of man in the New Testament is on the "spirit." Why? In the New Testament, under the New Covenant, man's spirit becomes most important because it is the receptacle of the Holy Spirit. To put it another way, our spirit is the living environment in which the Holy Spirit lives and works. The Holy Spirit didn't live totally, completely, permanently in followers of God under the Old Covenant. The Spirit came and went upon the judges of Israel (Judges 3:10; 6:34; 11:29; 14:6). The Spirit came and left Saul (1 Sam. 11:6 and 16:14). David, when he sinned with Bathsheba, feared that the Spirit would be taken from him as it had Saul (Psalm 51:11). The Spirit would "come upon" or "fill" a person for a particular role or function. The beauty of the New Covenant promise, which Peter recited from the book of Joel, "In the last days I will pour out My Spirit on all flesh."

My belief is that when a person begins to turn to Christ, it is because their spirit is being wooed or stirred or spoken to. If a person only comes to Christ because their mind is the only thing activated or only comes to Christ in an extremely emotional moment or event, that "conversion" will be short-lived (swayed by the next intellectual argument or the next emotional event) unless the transaction has taken place in their spirit.

Psa. 103:1 Bless the LORD, O my soul,
   And all that is within me, bless His holy name.
   2 Bless the LORD, O my soul, and forget none of His benefits;

David (the spirit of David) is commanding his soul to "get in line."

Jesus says in Matt. 10:28 "Do not fear those who kill the

body but are unable to kill the soul; but rather fear Him who is able to destroy both soul and body in hell."
Jesus is saying that God, the Father, can destroy both soul and body in hell. It is the spirit that is eternal. Jesus doesn't say that the Father destroys spirit and body but "soul and body."

Peter, in 1 Pet. 2:11, says, "Beloved, I urge you as aliens and strangers to abstain from fleshly lusts which wage war against the soul."

Peter is saying that the fleshly lusts through the body, are warring there in the soul. My soul is the battleground. The question is am I going to allow these lusts control my soul or allow my spirit (empowered by the Holy Spirit) to wage war against the things that are waging war against me. Or will I allow these lusts to have the victory?

OUR HEART

In Hebrew it's *leb*; in Greek it's *cardia*.

Psa. 9:1 I will give thanks to the LORD with all my heart;
	I will tell of all Your wonders.

One of the Beatitudes:

Matt. 5:8 "Blessed are the pure in heart, for they shall see God.

Paul says to Timothy: 1 Tim. 1:5 But the goal of our instruction is love from a pure heart and a good conscience and a sincere faith.

What is the distinction between spirit and heart? Sometimes, they look very much alike. The spirit is the innermost part of us. It is the receptacle of the Holy Spirit when we accept Christ and his work. But every person (we mentioned Pharaoh; also, in the book of Daniel, the scriptures say that the pagan king Nebuchadnezzar was 'troubled in his spirit') has a spirit. The spirit can be a receptacle and "meeting place" for other spirits as well as the Holy Spirit. The heart, on the other hand, is the center of convictions. One of the levels of meaning of the Hebrew word for heart (*leb*) means "the authority of the house". In other words, what convictions are governing me? We all live out of our convictions — the things we are convinced of. The heart is the seat of those convictions.

Where is our "heart?" I definitely do not believe it is in our soul. If we take this man-as-3-part scheme, then our heart must be in our spirit.

There are many scriptures where heart and spirit are closely connected:
Psa. 51:10 Create in me a clean heart, O God,
   And renew a steadfast spirit within me.
Psa. 51:17 The sacrifices of God are a broken spirit;
   A broken and a contrite heart, O God, You will not despise.
Psa. 77:6 I will remember my song in the night;
   I will meditate with my heart,
   And my spirit ponders:
Psa. 143:4 Therefore my spirit is overwhelmed within me;
   My heart is appalled within me.
Prov. 15:13 A joyful heart makes a cheerful face,
   But when the heart is sad, the spirit is broken.
Prov. 17:22 A joyful heart is good medicine,
   But a broken spirit dries up the bones.
Heb. 4:12 For the word of God is living and active and sharper than any two-edged sword, and piercing as far as the division of soul and spirit, of both joints and marrow, and able to

judge the thoughts and intentions of the heart.

In several of these passages it looks like the heart and the spirit are synonymous. However, look more closely at, say the first verse here quoted, Psalm 51:10. David is requesting that God do two different operations, one on his heart ("create") and another on his spirit ("renew"). Creating and renewing are two different activities.

In Proverbs 15:13 when the heart is "sad" it doesn't say that the spirit is sad; it says that the spirit is "broken."

In Hebrews 4, once the word has divided the soul and spirit, it judges the heart (in my estimation, a part of our spirit).

Perhaps I'm splitting hairs. I do see a distinction in some passages. However, we can consider our "heart" to be intimately connected with or part of our "spirit." When Jesus gives the "Great Commandment" (Matt. 22:37) He does not mention the spirit. He says, "You shall love the Lord your God with all your heart, with all our soul, with all your mind, and with all your strength."

He's not talking about the container (spirit) but about our convictions (heart). Our convictions come out of the container. He wants the Holy Spirit to influence our hearts so that we will have the convictions He wants us to have so that we will love God with all of it!

The Lord wants the Holy Spirit to so fill us that our spirit becomes the same with the Holy Spirit: 1 Cor. 6:17 But the one who joins himself to the Lord is one spirit with Him. Notice that in this version (NASB) "with Him" is in italics. This means that these two words aren't in the Greek translation. This verse should read, "But the one who joins himself to the Lord is one spirit." One spirit...our spirit so filled with His Spirit that it is one unity, identical.

If it is so important that we be "spiritual", will we commit ourselves to it?

There is a wonderful example of the importance of being spiritual in Acts 6, where there's a problem of people getting fed. The people who are to do something about the problem (the first deacons?) are to be "full of the spirit". How do you determine if a person is "full of the spirit"? How do you measure that? What does that look like? They chose Stephen, a man "full of faith and full of the Holy Spirit." Apparently this quality of being "full of the Holy Spirit" was observable! What if we still had these qualifications in our churches today for those who are to wait tables and be servants to the church!?!

OUR MIND

The Hebrew word most often translated "mind" in our English Old Testament is the word for "heart." In other words, the Hebrew mindset includes the idea that what we think originates in our heart, the seat of our convictions. Also, another word translated "mind" is the Hebrew word for "kidneys." Why? The kidneys were these organs deep down inside. The Hebrew mindset (as opposed to the Greek mindset) believed that the kidneys are the place that our deepest emotions emanated from, and, also, that deep emotion is the END result of a response of obedience, not the motivation for obedience. Consequently, the "mind" part of the human makeup that, finally, propels us into action:

Examine me, O LORD, and try me;
Test my mind and my heart. (Ps. 26:2)

In the Greek mindset, the mind is the pinnacle of human existence. Consequently, the acquisition of knowledge and of wisdom was the highest goal. The apostle Paul attacks such a mindset in 1 Corinthians 1:

> Where is the wise man? Where is the scribe? Where is the debater of this age? Has not God made foolish the wisdom of the world? For since in the wisdom of God the world through its wisdom did not come to know God, God was well-pleased through the foolishness of the message preached to save those who believe. For indeed Jews ask for signs and Greeks search for wisdom; but we preach Christ crucified, to Jews a stumbling block and to Gentiles foolishness, but to those who are the called, both Jews and Greeks, Christ the power of God and the wisdom of God. (vv. 21-24)

The mind is not, however, an inherently evil thing. Again, God has created us with minds that should worship Him:

> <u>Matt. 22:37</u> And He said to him, "' YOU SHALL LOVE THE LORD YOUR GOD WITH ALL YOUR HEART, AND WITH ALL YOUR SOUL, AND WITH ALL YOUR MIND.'

> <u>Rom 7:25</u> Thanks be to God through Jesus Christ our Lord! So then, on the one hand I myself with my **mind** am serving the law of God, but on the other, with my flesh the law of sin.

Often, in the Old Testament, the mind is connected with the term "heart" (Psalm 16:9). But, often, the mind is separated from the soul. Why? I believe it is because of the importance of the mind as one of the primary battlegrounds in which our enemy strikes. Also, the mind is the "place" in which we spend so much of our time.

But, as I've said before, the issue is: what is CONTROLLING my mind!

OUR FLESH

In the Old Testament the word "flesh" either denoted the physical body of the individual or humankind in general (i.e., Gen. 6:12; Psalm 38:7). Jesus, and then the writers of the New Testament, however, introduced the concept of the "flesh" being the sinful prerogative of living life out of our own resources instead of availing ourselves of the resources of our heavenly Father:

> Matt 26:41" Keep watching and praying that you may not enter into temptation; the spirit is willing, but the flesh is weak."

> Rom 8:6 For the mind set on the flesh is death, but the mind set on the Spirit is life and peace...

OUR COMPLEX NATURE

In summarizing, there are several passages in which some or all of these "parts" of our nature are brought together:

> Mark 12:30-31
> AND YOU SHALL LOVE THE LORD YOUR GOD WITH ALL YOUR HEART, AND WITH ALL YOUR SOUL, AND WITH ALL YOUR MIND, AND WITH ALL YOUR STRENGTH.'

1 Thess 5:23-24
Now may the God of peace Himself sanctify you entirely; and may your spirit and soul and body be preserved complete, without blame at the coming of our Lord Jesus Christ.

Heb. 4:12
For the word of God is living and active and sharper than any two-edged sword, and piercing as far as the division of soul and spirit, of both joints and marrow, and able to judge the thoughts and intentions of the heart.

Hence, Scripturally,
1. Man (mankind/womankind) is composed, in general terms, of two parts: an outer man (body, flesh) and an inner man.
2. Whereas the O.T. uses the term "flesh" strictly in the physical sense, Jesus and the writers of the N.T. sometimes broaden that term to include our fallen nature apart from God and all that it relies upon other than Him (our sinful self, fallen nature). Either usage always shows man in weakness or being transitory:

- Gen. 6:13 Then God said to Noah, " The end of all flesh has come before Me; for the earth is filled with violence because of them; and behold, I am about to destroy them with the earth.

- Isa. 40:6 A voice says, "Call out." Then he answered, "What shall I call out?" All flesh is grass, and all its loveliness is like the flower of the field.

- Matt. 26:41 " Keep watching and praying that you may not enter into temptation; the spirit is willing, but the flesh is weak."

- The body may refer to the human body or be used metaphorically as in 1 Cor. 12.
3. The inner man is referred to in many ways. In the O.T. the emphasis is upon the *nephesh*, the soul, that part of us that makes us "alive"; it's the seat of appetites, the emotions, the will and moral activity. The "heart" is similar but usually refers to how/where our commitment lies, our inward motivations (One of the meanings of the Hebrew word for heart, *leb*, is "the authority of the house"). The "spirit" of man in the O.T. appears, many times, as synonymous with the "soul". But *ruach*, the spirit, in man is never used for "life."

4. In the N.T. things changed somewhat. The usage of "heart" stays pretty much the same, but the spirit of man overpowers the soul. The spirit comes into the forefront, undoubtedly, because the spirit becomes the receptacle of the Holy Spirit. From the spirit springs the passion, the heart for the Lord. Within the spirit is communion and communication with and from the Lord:

- 1 Cor. 2:9-11 (v. 14 – "but the natural man [psyche = soulish])

- Romans 8:16 The Spirit Himself testifies with our spirit that we are children of God,

- 2 Tim 4:22 The Lord be with your spirit. Grace be with you

All of our "parts" function together, each having an effect upon the others. But, if our Lord desires that we live "spiritually", then we must begin to cultivate an awareness, a sensitivity, to our spirit and to the activity of the Holy Spirit within our spirits.

The typical drawing to illustrate the three parts of man is:

The way we operate day-to-day, however, is very different:

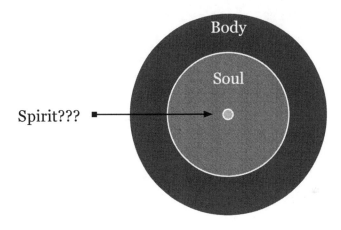

In my 43 years of Christian living, I've been taught quite a bit about the Holy Spirit. And I've taught that the Holy Spirit lives inside of me, to control me. But where the Spirit lives and what the Spirit does, and how I (in spirit) may cooperate with the Spirit of God has only recently been emphasized.

Here is my proposal for living spiritually:

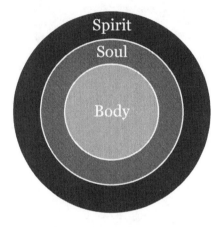

We must live BIG spiritually! We must live DEEPLY! We must live "from deep within." We must be aware of our spirit and what it does: the topic of our next chapter.

SUMMARY

- We are created with an "outer man" and an "inner man"
- In the Old Testament we see the operation of the spirit in both believers and non-believers
- There is more emphasis in the Old Testament on our soul.
- There is more emphasis in the New Testament on our spirit.
- There are differences in the terms "spirit", "soul", "heart", "mind", and "flesh"
- All of our "parts" (spirit, soul, and body) have an affect on one another
- We must live "big"!

Questions

1. Do you spend more time thinking about your "inner man" or your "outer man"?
2. Have you (the real you, the spiritual you) ever command your soul to "get in line"?
3. How aware are you of activity in your spirit?

Chapter Four

WHAT DOES OUR SPIRIT DO?

A number of years ago a young friend of mine was going on a mission trip overseas. As I drove him to the airport, I was "impressed" to give him the cash that was in my wallet. When we arrived at the drop off I gave him the money. He then told me, as he looked at the amount, that it was the exact amount he was "short" for the trip. What "impressed" or "motivated" me to give the money? We can answer in general terms, "the Lord impressed me to do that." But how, did the Lord impress me?

We have been created with these three "parts" — spirit, soul, and body. But it is my argument that we are more aware of the function of our souls (intellect, emotions, willpower) and of our bodies. How aware are we of the function of our spirit? I've not had much teaching, in my Christian walk, about my spirit. So let's look, again, to the Scriptures to see how our spirit is designed to operate. What does our spirit do?

THE MOTIVATOR

Exodus 35:21 Everyone whose heart stirred him and everyone whose spirit moved him came and brought the LORD'S contribution for the work of the tent of meeting and for all its service and for the holy garments.

This first verse describes the building of the Tabernacle in the wilderness and the gathering of resources for its construction. The "heart" was "stirred" and the "spirit" was "moved." Their spirit was willing.

Ezra 1:5 Then the heads of fathers' households of Judah and

Benjamin and the priests and the Levites arose, even everyone whose spirit God had stirred to go up and rebuild the house of the LORD which is in Jerusalem.

In the return of the exiles back to the land from Babylon, this description is that their "heart" (*ruach* = spirit, in Hebrew) was "moved" to return.

Negatively, the next verse will make the same point:

Zeph. 1:12
"It will come about at that time
That I will search Jerusalem with lamps,
And I will punish the men
Who are stagnant in spirit,
Who say in their hearts,
'The LORD will not do good or evil!'

Here we see that the spirit can be "stagnant." This is a spirit that is not moved!

From these verses we see that our spirit is a "catalyst"; it is a motivator. One of the functions of our spirit is to motivate or move us into action, to get us going (Incidentally, in Romans 12 the apostle Paul is describing what a community of faith is to look like. In verse 11, he says they are to be "fervent in spirit." The Greek word for "fervent" is *zeo*. It means "to bubble, to boil." Our spirit is to be stirred up, moved, and boiling!).

THE PONDERER

Psalm 77:6
I will remember my song in the night;
I will meditate with my heart,
And my spirit ponders:

"My spirit ponders (NASB)." This Hebrew word for "ponder" is so very interesting. It means to search for something hidden and not give up until you find it. The function of our spirit is to ponder, to search deep and hidden things.

Proverbs 20:27
>   The spirit of man is the lamp of the LORD,
>   Searching all the innermost parts of his being.

Here the spirit functions as a lamp, illuminating and searching the deep parts of my being. Like a large flashlight in an underground cavern I am seeking what is there. I am searching for the deep things that are in me (both the helpful and unhelpful) and for the deep things the Lord desires to reveal to me. Our spirit is a ponderer, a searcher, a meditator.

Let me try to get as practical as I can. For instance, when I am reading Scripture, having a devotional time with the Lord, and I come upon a "zinger" — one of those verses or passages to which I respond, "Wow!", one which "gets me", one which just "climbed into my Bible" ("I didn't know that was there!"). What I will do, how I will respond, is to close my eyes and I will try to get that point, that truth, that encounter with the word, from my mind down into my spirit. I will let it begin to tumble in my spirit. I will let my spirit begin to search it out, to ponder it. "Lord, I want to squeeze every little drop out of this living word You've given me."

Isaiah 26:9
>   At night my soul longs for You,
>   Indeed, my spirit within me seeks You diligently;
>   For when the earth experiences Your judgments
>   The inhabitants of the world learn righteousness.

This is similar to "ponder", a searching. However, the verses above speak of searching the THINGS of God whereas this verse speaks of searching for God HIMSELF.

THE COUNSELOR

Malachi 2:15
" But not one has done so who has a remnant of the Spirit. And what did that one do while he was seeking a godly offspring? Take heed then to your spirit, and let no one deal treacherously against the wife of your youth.

Take heed to your spirit (NIV, "guard your spirit") means that our spirit gives counsel, advice, or it functions to give us discernment. As a New Testament believer, then, indwelt by the Holy Spirit with Him in control, our spirit becomes the place to receive counsel from Him. "Discernment" has more of an intuitive aspect; "counsel" has more of an informational aspect. The Holy Spirit, operating in our spirit, can give both.

To further our understanding, there are many Hebrew words for "discernment." Two of the main Hebrew words are *ta'amim* and *binyah*. *Binyah* has, as it's Hebrew base, the letters b-n which mean "son." In other words, we can see God giving us, even in the Old Testament, a foretaste that all discernment only comes through His son, Jesus the Messiah. The other word, *ta'amim*, has the idea of circling a situation and seeing it from all directions. It means that we look at a person, an idea, a situation at hand and see it in a 360° perspective, looking at every aspect of it.

THE PERCEIVER

Mark 2:8 Immediately Jesus, aware in His spirit that they were reasoning that way within themselves, said to them, "Why are you reasoning about these things in your hearts?

Jesus "perceived" something in His spirit. What did He perceive? He perceived something that other people were thinking but not saying, and He perceived it in His spirit. You may read this (and many other passages in the gospels) and say, "He was the Son of God; I'm not. So, I can't do that." I used to do that for the first 16 or 17 years of my life as the follower of Jesus. But I don't do that anymore. One of the reasons is that I look at Jesus as my role model. Jesus laid aside His godly attributes (Philippians 2:5-8) and came to us as a man, fully dependent upon the Holy Spirit. He is our role model of someone who was always controlled by the Spirit. Jesus was always a spiritual person.

So our spirit is the place where we perceive things, things that we cannot know otherwise, an activity that is beyond natural ways of knowing and understanding, beyond our natural senses. Our spirit is a place where we get information in supernatural ways.

THE REJOICER

Luke 1:46 And Mary said: "my soul exalts the Lord, 47 And my spirit has rejoiced in God my Savior."

"My soul exalts the Lord." In present tense time, Mary is exalting the Lord. But her spirit "has rejoiced." That's past tense. In other words, Mary's spirit rejoiced before her soul exalted. There was an activity of her spirit, first, that caused or resulted in exaltation from her soul. One of the functions of our spirits, then, is to rejoice, to be a place of rejoicing.

THE STRENGTHENER

Luke 1:80 And the child continued to grow and to become strong in spirit, and he lived in the deserts until the day of his public appearance to Israel.

"And the child ..." Which child? In the context of the passage, the child is John the Baptist and his spirit was strengthened. Our spirit can be strengthened. Our spirit can get stronger. There are activities and ways in which we can participate with God so that our spirit can be stronger.

John 4:23 "But an hour is coming, and now is, when the true worshipers will worship the Father in spirit and truth; for such people the Father seeks to be His worshipers. 24 "God is spirit, and those who worship Him must worship in spirit and truth."

One of the primary functions of our spirit is to worship. The word "worship" comes from the combination of two English terms: worth + ship. It means the quality of worth, or value. True worship is a revelation and response to the knowing the "value" of God. Our spirit can recognize this value of the Lord and respond with adoration and love.

In addition to these functions or activities of our spirit, listed below are others"

- our spirits can be broken or crushed *Ps. 34:18; Prov. 15:4*
- our spirits can be provoked, disturbed *John 11:33; Acts 17:16*
- our spirit can be refreshed *2 Cor. 7:13*
- our spirit can be overwhelmed (Heb. "fainted") *Ps. 142:3*
- our spirit can be/should be fervent (on fire) *Romans 12:13*
- our spirit can receive a witness, a testimony *Romans 8:16*
- our spirit can be/should be joined with the H.S. *1 Cor. 6:17*
- our spirit can serve *Rom. 1:9*
- our spirit is our life *Lk. 23:46; Acts 7:59*

Our spirit is a living and active part of us. Often we have

minimized, overlooked or ignored our spirit. Our spirit can act and be acted upon more than we think. It can be responsive to things and people around us. The spirit can be the command headquarters for God in our lives. The Holy Spirit lives where? In our spirit. We are the temple of God; He lives in our spirit.

Again, we see this in the picture of the tabernacle or temple pattern: the outer court (our body), the inner room (our soul), and the holy of holies, the residence of God (our spirit). We see this explained in Hebrews 9 and 10. The writer of Hebrews is explaining how this new covenant enabled and inaugurated by Jesus is better than the old covenant. He reminds the reader of the configuration of the tabernacle: outer court, holy place, and holy of holies (including the articles placed in each place). He reminds the reader who was allowed in the holy place (priests) and who was allowed in the holy of holies (only the high priest, once a year). He explains that Jesus, as both sacrifice and high priest, has entered the true holy of holies, God's presence, and is continually before Him. Then, in verses 19 through 25 of chapter 10, the author sets up this sequence:

"Therefore,...(the conclusion or result of Jesus' work/ministry explained in this argument)

...since we have confidence to enter the holy place by the blood of Jesus...

"since we have a great high priest . . .

let us draw near...
let us hold fast...
let us consider how to stimulate..."

What is this author telling us? The tabernacle and priestly function under the old covenant were a picture for us today. The tabernacle, the place where the presence of God is, now is our spirit (1 Cor. 3:16). Because of what Jesus has done (sacrifice) and is now doing (high priestly function of continually presenting to God His sacrificial blood) we can go "in" to the presence of God. Where? In our spirit. "Draw near" ... go in ... to His presence with boldness.

Sometimes when we Christians have a good worship experience at a church meeting, we may say, "Wow, we were really in the presence of God today!" And that may be true. Worship (and what we have come to mean by "worship" is singing spiritual songs and the experience that comes with that) is truly a way to enter His presence. But Monday morning, sitting at your breakfast table, you can go "in", into His presence. God must be worshipped in spirit (and in truth). He is always there. So often, however, we are out of touch with Him. Many times it is almost like the thick veil is still there (as it was between the Holy place and the Holy of Holies). And we think He is back there someplace behind the curtain and we aren't in touch. But the writer of Hebrews is saying, "Go in!"

Often, these functions and activities of our spirit can be short-circuited or even quenched. Over the years when someone has brought criticism or evaluation to my life, I have not lived out of my spirit but out of my soul: rationalizing, reacting emotionally. But, I've learned a few things. Years ago some friends came, bringing criticisms of my wife and me. What we tried to do in that period of time was to hear and respond from our spirit. We listened and asked the Lord, "OK, Lord, what, of these things they are saying, is true and what is not?" Almost in every case, we found there were things that were true and that required, "I was wrong. Forgive me." Many times we are shut down by the way a person acts; they are irritating; they don't bring the information in a loving way. But, if we respond from our spirit, controlled by the Holy Spirit, then we can see that, sometimes as my wife says, "God brings us a Christmas present wrapped in barbed wire!"

Our spirit is such a fascinating part of us. It is the "real" us. Paul says that when this "tent" which is our body is torn down, we have a "building" in the heavens where the real "we" will be present with the Lord.

It has always been helpful for me to see spiritual truths lived out through a human being. I've had many role models who have encouraged me to take hold of more (all?) of what I've been made to be and do. In the next chapter let's look at the person who best exemplifies a spiritual person.

SUMMARY

- Our spirit can motivate us to accomplish God's will
- Our spirit can ponder (search) out the things of God
- Our spirit can be the place where we take counselor or get discernment
- Our spirit functions in many other ways according to Scripture

Questions

1. When is the last time you can recall that you were "moved" by your spirit?
2. Deep within, are you seeking the Lord Himself?
3. What do you think He means when Jesus says, "God is spirit; those who worship Him must worship in spirit and in truth"?

Chapter Five

THE MODEL SPIRITUAL PERSON

I have, buried somewhere in a box or file, a picture of me standing next to my father. I remember where it was taken. I was four (maybe five) years old. It was summertime. In those days (early 1950's) most people mowed their yards with a push lawnmower. In the picture my dad is standing behind the mower, with its wooden handle and metal blades. Right next to him is me. I'm behind my little white plastic mower. Both of us standing tall. Both of us ready to mow.

I'm telling you about my picture because it illustrates the point of this chapter: we all need a role model. To be what we are created to be and to do what we've been created to do is helped when we see someone who's "been there; done that."

What does a spiritual person look like? Who is our best model of a man living out of his spirit? Jesus is, of course. He's "been there; done that." So let's look at some examples from Jesus' life on earth when He lived out of His spirit.

THE SPIRIT REMAINING

John 1:32 John testified saying, " I have seen the Spirit descending as a dove out of heaven, and He remained upon Him."

Even in Old Testament believers, the Holy Spirit came upon and came off of judges, priests, kings, and selected other individuals. We see this in King Saul's life; the Spirit came upon Saul but also, later, departed. When David sinned with the Uriah/Bathsheba affair, he was afraid that God's Spirit would depart from him (Psalm 51:11).

But, here, John the Baptist's testimony is that with Jesus, who is ushering in this new kingdom-of-God-way-of-living, the Spirit remains. Interestingly enough, John saw this; he recognized this supernatural occurrence. Perhaps, John, from his Old Testament point of view, was surprised! So this is the first thing we see in the interaction of Jesus with the Spirit – it came and remain and stayed with Him during the rest of His life and ministry on earth.

Most of my Christian life, I was taught and believed that when I see Jesus in the gospels, performing miracles, walking by the Spirit, the emphasis was He was the Son of God. He was and is. But seeing Him ONLY as the Son of God caused me to "write off" or diminish His life as an example. In other words, I would read that Jesus healed the sick. My response was, "Well, He was God and I'm not, so I can't do that." I would read passages in which Jesus did things by the Spirit and say, "Well, He was God and although I have the Holy Spirit I can only do 2% of what Jesus did." I negated the fact that Jesus came not only to save me from my sins but also to show me how to live out of my spirit, by the Holy Spirit.

Why was John able to see this supernatural "falling" of the Holy Spirit upon Jesus? For our sake! So that we can see Him receiving the Spirit and walking by the Spirit Who remains and, likewise, receive and walk by the same Spirit ourselves!

LED BY THE SPIRIT

<u>Matt. 4:1</u> Then Jesus was led up by the Spirit into the wilderness to be tempted by the devil.

Matthew is writing, basically, to the Jews to prove that Jesus is the Messiah, the king of the Jews. There are more Old Testament references in Matthew than in any other gospel. The Biblical symbolism of kingship is the lion. The God of Israel and Jesus are depicted as a lion (Hos. 11:10; Rev. 5:5). Mark writes and shows us Jesus as the servant, the one who bears our burdens, Mark 10:45 (like an ox in Biblical times). Therefore, Mark is the gospel of action. "Immediately" is used 40 times in Mark. There is a lot of movement and serving in Mark.

Why am I pointing this out here? In this passage in Matthew 4, the verb for the activity of the Spirit is "led up." But when Mark describes the same event, he uses the Greek word which means "thrust out" ("impelled" in NASB). In Matthew, the Spirit leads Jesus into the wilderness. In Mark, Jesus is thrown out into the wilderness. Have you ever had the activity of the Holy Spirit so strong in your life that you feel "thrown out"?

Digressing for a minute: to finish with the differing presentations of Jesus in the gospels, Luke presents Jesus as a man. Luke (writing as the physician he was) points out the human responses of Jesus more than the other gospel writers. Luke is much more interested in Jesus' conception and birth. He is the only writer to refer to Jesus' years between His birth and baptism (Luke 2:39-52). It is in Luke that we see Jesus weeping over Jerusalem (Luke 19:41). In the gospel of John, Jesus is presented as the Son of God (John is very clear about this in 20:31). Jesus is presented from the "heavenly" aspect of His nature.

In both Ezekiel (1:5-10) and the Revelation (chapter 4:6,7) the prophet and the apostle see the spiritual environment surrounding the person/throne of God. Here, among so many other amazing things, they both see creatures that have the face of a lion (king), an ox (servant), a man (humanity), and an eagle (heavenly). These are the four presentations of Jesus in the four gospels.

SPIRITUAL WARFARE

<u>Matt. 12:28</u> "But if I cast out demons by the Spirit of God, then the kingdom of God has come upon you.

What was Jesus doing by the Spirit of God? He was casting out demons. We cannot do spiritual warfare without the Spirit operating in our spirit. You cannot do successful spiritual warfare in your soul. You cannot outthink a demon. You cannot cast out a demon by getting angry. Yelling at a demonic presence does not have any more effect than whispering to one (I know by experience: both yelling and whispering). Paul reminds us in 2 Corinthians 10:4 that the weapons of our warfare are not fleshly, carnal. They are "divinely powerful." That is, they are spiritual. And spiritual weapons must be utilized in, by, and through the spirit.

We are given a story in Acts 19:13-17 about 7 men who thought they would take on an evil spirit in another man. They thought that they could just say some words, like a magic mantra, and the demon would leave. The demon's reply is classic: "I recognize Jesus, and I know about Paul, but who are you?" I believe this evil presence was recognizing the spirituality of both Jesus and Paul. The rest of the story tells of this demonized man overcoming and stripping the seven. The result is hallmark: "This became known to all, both Jews and Greeks, who lived in Ephesus; and fear fell upon them all and the name of the Lord Jesus was being magnified" (verse 17). There was a spiritual lesson learned here: Jesus, and the ones who are inhabited by Him, are the spiritual victors.

"But who are you?" I don't ever want a demon to say that to me! I want to be so filled with the Spirit in my spirit that I will have a reputation not only in heaven but also in the realms of darkness. Most Christians I've talked to have a fear of demons. If and when the demonic manifests itself they don't want to have anything to do with it. But I like what the late John Wimber used to say, "I don't see a demon behind every bush; but when I meet one, I don't beat around the bush!" Greater is He Who is in us than He who is in the world (1 John 4:4)!

AWARE IN OUR SPIRITS

<u>Mark 2:8</u> Immediately Jesus, aware in His spirit that they were reasoning that way within themselves, said to them, "Why are you reasoning about these things in your hearts?

In this story about the paralytic being healed after he was lowered through the roof, the religious leaders are offended by Jesus' pronouncement of forgiveness and "reasoning in their hearts,..." They were thinking things but not verbalizing them in this scene. However, Jesus perceived what they were thinking. Where did He perceive them? Our verse says "aware in His spirit." Jesus knew what was going on in His spirit. Our spirit can be like an antenna picking up signals that are not communicated in the natural realm. I know several people who, when they walk into a room or into a restaurant must either walk out again or sit where they cannot see many people. The reason is that they are "picking up" what is going on in people all over the room. Probably most of us don't want to get that sensitive. But this aspect of spiritual living is very helpful when you are trying to help, encourage, and minister to others. Sometimes people cannot verbalize what is going on with them. Or perhaps they are too scared to verbalize it. The Lord can give a "short cut" and enable us to get to the point of praying and bringing the presence of God into their problems.

I have told of the prayer session with a young woman in my book, <u>Kingdom Come! Tales of a Supernatural God</u>. This woman had come to the prayer group asking for prayer about some emotional problems she was having. After speaking with her for a few minutes, the group bowed their heads to prayer for her. I had been trained to keep my eyes opened when I pray for others to see (either in the natural or in the spirit) what was going on. I began to "see" on this woman's cheek, a word. It looked as if she had been out in the sun all day but had tape forming a word across her cheek. All of the rest of her face had flesh color, but this "word" was white and clear and distinct. The word was "resentment." So I stopped the prayer and said, "Excuse me, but before we pray can I ask you a question? Do you have resentment against anyone?" The woman began to cry and related a deep resentment she felt toward her mother. We all helped her to come to the place of granting forgiveness to her mother. Guess what? Her emotional problems went away! As I've said, ministering out of our spirit (led by the Holy Spirit) can be quite helpful!

This doesn't happen to me all of the time. There are many times praying for people that I look and I get nothing. But we have this constant potential of operating out of our spirit the way Jesus did. I believe Jesus walked around with His "radar" operating. This occasion was not the only time that He knew what was going on without someone telling Him. This is another application (for us) of the truth that when we join ourselves to the Lord we are one spirit with Him (1 Cor. 6:17). Jesus' spirit was one with the Holy Spirit (as our is). When the Holy Spirit controls our spirit we participate in these kinds of spiritual activities.

GROANING IN THE SPIRIT

<u>Mark 8:12</u> Sighing deeply in His spirit, He said, "Why does this generation seek for a sign? Truly I say to you, no sign will be given to this generation."

Twice in the gospels, Jesus "sighs": here and in Mark 7 when He heals the man who was deaf and spoke with difficulty. The word means to sigh, groan, or pray fervently internally. The other significant use of this word is found in Romans 8:23 and 26 where it speaks of the activity of groaning "within ourselves" and the groanings brought about by the intercessory ministry of the Holy Spirit. In Jesus' spirit was a groaning, a moaning, a deep, intercessory activity. There was, I believe, in this encounter with the religious leaders who were asking for a sign, a kind of "you've got to be kidding Me" kind of reaction starting in Jesus' spirit. Similarly, in John 11:33, when Jesus came to Lazarus' tomb and saw Mary and the people weeping, He was "deeply moved in spirit and was troubled." Also, in the upper room: John 13:21 When Jesus had said this, He became troubled in spirit, and testified and said, "Truly, truly, I say to you, that one of you will betray Me."

These are all activities taking place in the spirit of Jesus. His spirit sighed; it was moved; it was troubled. Have you ever had these experiences before? I have. I have had times when I knew that something was going on, deep inside, but I couldn't put a label on it. All I could say was that my spirit was being stirred up. Sometimes, later, I understood what was going on. At other times, I've never known what was happening. Either way, I believe my spirit was being activated at a level deeper than I could think or feel.

This happened to me recently during a trip to Herrnhut, Germany. Herrnhut is the location of the "Moravian Pentecost" during the 1700's. From an intense time of spiritual encounters with the Holy Spirit in Herrnhut, Moravian believers set in motion a continual, 100-year prayer session and sent missionaries all over the world. As we drove past the city limit sign into this village, I began to tremble and shake. My spirit was greatly "moved." This experience continued for the entire time (several hours) I was there. When we drove out of the village at the end of our brief stay, it stopped. It was only after several weeks had gone by a discerning sister gave me the understanding of what was taking place at a spirit level.

ANOINTED FOR MINISTRY

Luke 4:18 " THE SPIRIT OF THE LORD IS UPON ME, BECAUSE HE ANOINTED ME TO PREACH THE GOSPEL TO THE POOR. HE HAS SENT ME TO PROCLAIM RELEASE TO THE CAPTIVES, AND RECOVERY OF SIGHT TO THE BLIND, TO SET FREE THOSE WHO ARE OPPRESSED, 19 TO PROCLAIM THE FAVORABLE YEAR OF THE LORD."

Jesus, our "role model," was filled in His spirit with this anointing of the Holy Spirit for carrying out His kingdom agenda (in His spirit was the Holy Spirit empowering Him to perform each of these "categories"). These five "categories": preaching the gospel to the poor, proclaiming release to the captives, recovery of sight to the blind, setting free the oppressed, and proclaiming the favorable year of the Lord (the year of jubilee in which all debts are cancelled), are all accomplished as we read Luke's account of Jesus' life and ministry.

The question subsequently arises, "How much of our ministry, using these five categories as our guide, is out of our soul versus out of our spirit empowered by the Holy Spirit?" I'm not saying we don't use our minds or feel with our feelings or make choices as we minister to people. But, as I've said before, are our minds informing our spirit or our spirits informing our minds? If we are controlled by our spirit, then we can connect with people through a spirit-controlled soul.

The primary example of this is in the book of Acts, chapter 8. Philip has gone (because of persecution in Jerusalem) to the city of Samaria. Through his powerful preaching of the good news of the kingdom and demonstration of that kingdom in healings and deliverances, the entire city was stirred up and filled with joy. On day "whatever" of the revival going on there, Philip gets up for another powerful day and the Spirit speaks to him and tells him to leave and go to the desert to meet one man. This scenario in Samaria would be any pastor's, missionary's, or evangelist's dream! Yet the Spirit says to leave "Revival Town" and go to one man in a desert place. This wouldn't make sense to the human mind at the time. Now, looking back on this story, we can see God's reasons and timing. That one man took the gospel back to Africa. But back then, at the time, it might have seemed stupid, irresponsible. Yet here is a man whose ministry was controlled by the Spirit of God.

POWER FOR HEALING

Luke 5:17 One day He was teaching; and there were some Pharisees and teachers of the law sitting there, who had come from every village of Galilee and Judea and from Jerusalem; and the power of the Lord was present for Him to perform healing.

Why does Luke mention that "the power of the Lord was present for Him to perform healing"? Wasn't that power there every day? Why speak of it THAT day? Jesus, remember, has a spirit which is completely filled by the Holy Spirit. His spirit and the Spirit are one. There are two things which "draw" power out of Jesus. One is the activity of the Father ("I only do what I see the Father doing," which includes the movement of the Spirit within His spirit, i.e. compassion). The other is faith. Faith draws out the power of Jesus (cf. the woman with the hemorrhage, the Syro-Phoenician woman, and passages like Matt. 14:36). Remember, now, that Luke is a physician. He is extremely interested in human disease and the eradication of that disease. There are more examples in Luke of physical healing than in any other gospel.

Luke accompanied Paul on his journey to Jerusalem when Paul was arrested. Paul spent over two years in house arrest in Caesarea. I believe that it was during this time that Luke travelled Judea and Galilee interviewing "eye witnesses" (cf. Luke 1:2) of Jesus' life and ministry. Probably what he heard from those witnesses who were there that day with Jesus was "and the power of the Lord was present for Him to perform healing." Apparently, because of what we read elsewhere in the gospels, one or both of those ingredients (the Father's leading and/or faith) was present that day to "draw" out the wonder-working power of our Lord. This is speculation. But I think it is an "educated guess."

REJOICING IN THE SPIRIT

<u>Luke 10:21</u> At that very time He rejoiced greatly in the Holy Spirit, and said, "I praise You, O Father, Lord of heaven and earth, that You have hidden these things from the wise and

intelligent and have revealed them to infants. Yes, Father, for this way was well-pleasing in Your sight.

The context of this passage is that Jesus has sent out the 70 "missionaries" and they have come back to report. Jesus had sent them out to the villages with the instructions "and heal those in it who are sick, and say to them, 'The kingdom of God has come near to you.'" They had gone and it had happened! They came back pumped!

Let me digress for a moment. Jesus sent out seventy men. Any Old Testament passage that speaks of 70 men come to mind? Right! In Numbers 11 Moses is complaining to the Lord that he is having to deal with Israel alone. Moses was the justice of the peace, the criminal judge, and the court of appeals. But God has a plan. He tells Moses to gather for Him seventy men from the elders of Israel. He will put His Spirit on these men. They will bear the burden of the people alongside Moses. Jesus, among other things, presents Himself as the "new" Moses. And here He takes of the Spirit that is upon Him and places it on seventy others. This is the "new" Israel (those who believe in Him). These guys are the New Testament equivalent of the elders of Israel who will bear the load.

Now, with these returning missionaries, Jesus "rejoiced greatly in the Holy Spirit." Most of the time when I think about joy, I think about an emotion. Joy is an emotional "upper." But here it says that Jesus rejoiced "in the Holy Spirit." Is that different than the emotion of joy? I believe that "joy" might look the same, but that it comes from a different origin (either soul or spirit/Spirit). A soulish joy is, much of the time, connect to our happiness, to "happenings" (circumstances), to if things are going "well" for us, and to things that benefit us or someone close to us. Joy from the spirit/Spirit can be deeper and not even connected to happenings. I believe it is connected to the spiritual dynamics of faith, hope, love and truth.

As I was teaching and provoking believers in a home study with this material, a mother spoke of "releasing" her children to go to China as missionaries. She was sad, grieving with human emotion. Yet, in her spirit she was rejoicing that her children were following the Lord's leading.

THE IMMEASURABLE PROMISE

John 3:34 "For He whom God has sent speaks the words of God; for He gives the Spirit without measure."

What a promise! What a promise! This is John the Baptist speaking. He says that Jesus gives the Spirit without measure. There are no limits on how "much" of the Holy Spirit we can receive. There are historical accounts, through the centuries, of believers who have had intense experiences with the Holy Spirit. Some of these experiences were termed "ecstatic" experiences. It is said that Clare of Assisi, Francis de Sales, Teresa of Avila, Catherine of Sienna literally glowed after intense encounters with God. So many more have had encounters with a variety of experiences (of course all of these must pass mature discernment and support of the Word).

The apostle Paul, even after all of his experiences with the Lord (the many visions and conversations with Christ, healings, Paul speaking in tongues, casting out demons) said, toward the end of his life, essentially, "I want more" (Phil. 3:10-14) until he experienced the resurrection from the dead.

Many times when I am praying for myself or for others (when others come and ask for "more of the Spirit" or to be "filled with the Spirit" or whatever terminology they use) I will pray that the Lord will give us more than we think we can handle. I want to experience the Spirit "without measure"!

In our ministry on the streets here in Dallas, Texas, we have prayed for people to experience God. On several occasions, even with those who don't know Jesus yet, they have begun to tremble or feel "heavy" and they exclaim, "What is happening to me?" We just reply, "That's the presence of God, the presence of His Spirit." We can always ask for MORE! Don't ever be bashful for more. This is one of the few places in which you can be greedy and it's OK. God wants to give us more.

At this point, when I was presenting these truths to a small group, one man lamented that he, as a businessman, was so rationalistic and had relied on his mind almost exclusive. "I think a lot of my rational thinking limits the power of Christ. How do I get out of that?" he said. First, I was thrilled that this man was confronted by these truths and by this desire for an alternative way to live. I told him that I encourage Christian businessmen to change their thinking to offer up their businesses to become kingdom businesses. And I encourage them to establish at least these three kingdom principles: 1) Do everything out of love; 2) err on the side of generosity (be a giver); and 3) ask God about everything ... large and small.

The kingdom of God is what I call "the upside down kingdom." Take the way the world looks at things, what is normative for life (and business), and what "gets you ahead" and turn those principles and activities "upside down" and there you have how the kingdom operates. For example, the world says you "get" by "getting." The kingdom says you get by giving. The world says that the greatest is the boss, the kingdom says that the greatest is the servant. And so on. In today's world, in every arena — marketplace, politics, education, and even in the church — bigger is better. Yet, Jesus on many occasions, did His best to thin the crowd. We have our church growth programs. Jesus had His church-reduction program.

In exercising point number 3 above, asking God about everything, you may receive an answer like, "Use the business principle you learned at _____." , However, His answer may be doing something that doesn't look rational or wise at all, according to business principles. We just need to learn to listen to Him. Example: Jesus "had to pass through Samaria" to meet just one woman (at the well, John 4).

SUMMARIZING JESUS' MINISTRY

<u>Acts 10:37</u> you yourselves know the thing which took place throughout all Judea, starting from Galilee, after the baptism which John proclaimed. 38 " You know of Jesus of Nazareth, how God anointed Him with the Holy Spirit and with power, and how He went about doing good and healing all who were oppressed by the devil, for God was with Him.

The apostle Peter has been summoned to the house of Cornelius, a Jewish proselyte (a Gentile convert to Judaism). Cornelius was a righteous man and had a vision of an angel telling him to go get Peter at Joppa. Meanwhile, Peter is on the rooftop having a thrice-repeated vision. In this vision Peter hears the Lord tell him that what God has cleansed, no longer consider unholy. As Peter is coming out of his three visions three men from Cornelius are knocking at the door. Somewhere along the road from Joppa to Caesarea and

Cornelius' house Peter "gets it" – he understands the visions. Therefore he boldly walks into a foreigner's house (forbidden for a Jew under the Law) and begins to preach the gospel. In verse 38 Peter summarizes Jesus' entire earthly ministry from John's baptism up to His death. If you had just one sentence to tell someone about Jesus' earthly ministry, what would you say? Peter says that Jesus, anointed with the Spirit and with power, did good and healed. Now, he did go on to speak of the death and resurrection of Jesus and that "we are witnesses of all the things He did..." (verse 39).

Jesus lived and ministered by the Holy Spirit. The third person of the Trinity (Spirit) as He manifested Himself through the second person of the Trinity (Son) powerfully worked good and healed.

Our Father wants us to operate with the Holy Spirit and with power to do good and heal. Many times, what limits us is our unbelief and misplaced faith. Two good illustrations were given in our home study group. The first had to do with moving fluid from one container to another through an orifice. The lack of exercising our faith can close down the orifice. The other illustration was of purchasing a battery-operated toy. Many of these toys come with the battery but they have a clear plastic barrier over the battery terminals, which must be removed to operate and pull the power from the battery into the toy. The question is, can I remove the barrier. The battery (Holy Spirit, the source of power) is there all the time for a believer. What is or are the barriers that prevent me from receiving from the power source? This is what faith does. We will discuss the interaction of faith with living by the spirit/Spirit later.

Having looked at Jesus' life as the perfect example for us of someone who lived out of His spirit, we will now move on to answer the question, "Was Jesus able to pass this kind of living on to His followers, to us?"

SUMMARY

- Jesus is our best example of a spiritual person, One living out of His spirit.
- Jesus was continuously led by the Spirit.
- We cannot do "successful" spiritual warfare apart from living out of our spirit.
- We must do the works of Jesus empowered by the Spirit in our spirit.
- God gives His Spirit "without measure."
- The kingdom of God is an "upside down" kingdom to this world.

Questions

1. Do you believe that Jesus is our role model for spiritual living?
2. Do you think the demons would say, "I recognize Jesus, and I know about your name"?
3. Do you ever "sense" or "know" something that you would not know otherwise? Have you ever asked the Lord to hone this supernatural ability?
4. What do you think "rejoicing greatly in the Holy Spirit" would look like in your life?

Chapter Six

THE HOLY SPIRIT IN OUR SPIRIT

First, let's briefly look at other "role models," people in the New Testament, beginning in the gospels, who operated out of their spirit.

JOHN, ELIZABETH, MARY AND ZACHARIAS

In Luke 1 we are introduced to Zacharias, the husband of Elizabeth and future father of John, later called "the Baptist." In our passage Zacharias, a Levite who has, by lot, has received the job of going into the Holy Place in the temple to tend to the altar of incense and is confronted by an angel. This angel, who later identifies himself as Gabriel, prophesies to Zach about the birth and ministry of John. In that prophecy is verse 15:

"For he will be great in the sight of the Lord; and he will drink no wine or liquor, and he will be filled with the Holy Spirit while yet in his mother's womb.

We can see here that it is possible for a person to be filled with the Holy Spirit in their mother's womb. Even before the fetus fully develops or has a memory, he/she can receive the Holy Spirit. Pretty fascinating, huh? One application, of course, is for Christian parents to pray over the developing baby in the womb that he/she would be filled with the Spirit.

Elizabeth does, miraculously, become pregnant. In her last three months of pregnancy (compare v. 26 with v. 39) her relative Mary, who is now also pregnant with Jesus, goes for a visit. When Mary enters Elizabeth's house and gives a greeting we see, starting in Luke 1:41:

41 When Elizabeth heard Mary's greeting, the baby leaped in her womb; and Elizabeth was filled with the Holy Spirit. 42 And she cried out with a loud voice and said, "Blessed are you among women, and blessed is the fruit of your womb! 43 "And how has it happened to me, that the mother of my Lord would come to me? 44 "For behold, when the sound of your greeting reached my ears, the baby leaped in my womb for joy. 45 "And blessed is she who believed that there would be a fulfillment of what had been spoken to her by the Lord."

Elizabeth now is filled with the Holy Spirit. And the baby in her responds. It is a question whether little John responded to Mary's voice or whether he is responding to the presence of Jesus. Filled with the Spirit, Elizabeth now prophesies. She calls Mary "the mother of my Lord." She also mentions "a fulfillment of what had been spoken to her by the Lord." How did Elizabeth get this information? We don't know for sure. Perhaps Mary had written her an email or told her of the angelic visit and her impregnation by text message. But, perhaps, this is information that the Spirit of God is giving her at that moment. It certainly isn't beyond God to do just that.

Recently, we had a young pastor from Lima, Peru visiting our Sunday morning service. I had met him the previous evening at the home of one of our couples in the church. I had had only a brief conversation with him that night. But during the course of the Sunday meeting I received information from the Spirit and went to him to encourage him. I said, "I don't know what you will do with this but, if it is from the Lord, be encouraged. If it isn't throw it in the trash. But you are discipling a young man in his 20's. You are concerned whether or not he is ready to be released into ministry. The Lord says that he needs to continue to study the Scriptures. But the Lord says that even though you don't think he is ready, he is ready." The Peruvian pastor just stepped back and said, "Wow!" This was information I did not know. How did I then get this information? The Spirit of God released this info deep down in my spirit which was then communicated to my mind. I didn't receive a vision; I didn't hear a voice. I just "knew" some things in my spirit. Elizabeth just "knew" that Mary was carrying the Lord.

Luke 1:46 And Mary said:
" My soul exalts the Lord,
47 And my spirit has rejoiced in God my Savior.

The verb connected to "my soul" is present tense (exalts). The verb connected to "my spirit" is past tense (has rejoiced). In other words, Mary's spirit rejoiced before her soul exalted. The activity in her spirit produced or resulted in an activity in her soul.

Luke 1:67 And his father Zacharias was filled with the Holy Spirit, and prophesied, saying:

Now John has been born and Zacharias (muted by the Lord for his unbelief) comes into agreement with the Lord's word (John's name) and his mouth is opened by the Spirit and he begins to prophesy. The following prophecy is about the coming messiah. Wedged in the middle is another prophecy concerning John's coming ministry. Here the father is prophesying identity over his son.

SIMEON

Luke 2:25 And there was a man in Jerusalem whose name was Simeon; and this man was righteous and devout, looking for the consolation of Israel; and the Holy Spirit was upon him. 26 And it had been revealed to him by the Holy Spirit that he would not see death before he had seen the Lord's Christ. 27 And he came in the Spirit into the temple; and when the parents brought in the child Jesus, to carry out for Him the custom of the Law, 28 then he took Him into his arms, and blessed God, and said, 29 "Now Lord, You are releasing Your bond-servant to depart in peace, according to Your word; 30 For my eyes have seen Your salvation, 31 Which You have prepared in the presence of all peoples, 32 A LIGHT OF REVELATION TO THE GENTILES, And the glory of Your people Israel."

Here we see three activities of the Spirit in and with this man Simeon. First, the Holy Spirit was "upon him." This is similar to what we have seen in the Old Testament when the Spirit of God would be "upon" prophets, priests, and kings for them to carry out some activity of the Lord. Second, we see that the Spirit had "revealed" to Simeon some information. He wouldn't die until he had seen the Messiah. Third, Simeon, on a particular day at a particular moment, was moved by the Holy Spirit. It was as if the Spirit said, "Ok, get up right now and go to the temple! Right now!" As Simeon obeys he meets Joseph and Mary. The activity of the Spirit is timely. And, sometimes, many times, it is dependent upon our immediate obedience.

THE PROMISED ACTIVITY OF THE HOLY SPIRIT IN US

THE PROMISE OF HIS PRESENCE

In the so-called "Upper Room Discourse" (John 14-16) Jesus speaks often of the Holy Spirit. I don't know up to this point how much the disciples understood the working of the Holy Spirit in Jesus' life. They, of course, had seen him heal the sick and cast out demons. They had heard Him speak of the Spirit. Remember they were Jewish disciples. Disciples in the Jewish culture just didn't go sit in "discipleship classes", get up and go home. They went and lived with the rabbi. They not only wanted to know what the rabbi knew. They wanted to become like the rabbi ... in every way. I wonder if somewhere along the way, a disciple or a few of them began to ask, "How do we get this Holy Spirit? If He operates this way; we must operate this way." They had had a taste of the activity of the Spirit when Jesus sent them out on their mission (Matthew 10, Luke 9 and 10). But they could have believed that this impartation was temporary. But I believe a hunger and a thirst for more of the Spirit was created and if these hypothetical questions are close to what was going on, what Jesus tells them about the Holy Spirit in the upper room answers them.

In the context of John 14, Jesus, having just told his followers that He is leaving them, makes this great promise:

11 "Believe Me that I am in the Father and the Father is in Me; otherwise believe because of the works themselves. 12 "Truly, truly, I say to you, he who believes in Me, the works that I do, he will do also; and greater works than these he will do; because I go to the Father. 13 " Whatever you ask in My name, that will I do, so that the Father may be glorified in the Son. 14 "If you ask Me anything in My name, I will do it. John 14:15 " If you love Me, you will keep My commandments. 16 "I will ask the Father, and He will give you another Helper, that He may be with you forever; 17 that is the Spirit of truth, whom the world cannot receive, because it does not see Him or know Him, but you know Him because He abides with you and will be in you.

John 14:18 "I will not leave you as orphans; I will come to you. There is so much to see in these verses. It is the promise that Jesus will ask the Father to send the Holy Spirit to them. Jesus says (v. 17) that the Spirit will not just abide "with" them but will be "in" them. Jesus was "with" them. The Spirit is promised to be "in" them. And, I believe, this promise of the indwelling Holy Spirit connects with the promise of "greater works." How are they going to do greater works than Jesus, the works that He had done to that point of healing and delivering and proclaiming the kingdom? By the indwelling Spirit. Notice that (as I have been taught before) the greater works is not promised to a collective group. In other words, Jesus isn't promising that the church, collectively, will do greater works, as if the works can be "greater" because there are more of us than there was of Him. Jesus says, "he who believes in Me, the works that I do, he will do also; and greater works than these he will do; because I go to the Father." It's singular, not plural. It's in and through us as individual believers that the greater works are to take place.

Notice that connected to this promise of the Spirit in us is that "whatever you ask in My name, that will I do, so that the Father may be glorified in the Son. If you ask Me anything in My name, I will do it." I constantly remind the Lord of His words here. I tell Him that I am doing the best I can to live in the spirit/Spirit so that I know what His will is. Then I add, "You promised. You promised." I reminded the Lord one night as we were praying for a friend who had a brain tumor. She had had one tumor 5 years ago on one side of her brain. She had gone through treatment, along with being bathed in prayer. The tumor, a very dangerous and malignant type, had disappeared! Now, five years later, the same kind of tumor had appeared on the other side of the brain. We gathered together and prayed, and I prayed again, "Lord, You promised. You promised."

In John 14:16, quoted above, Jesus says He will ask for "another Helper" (i.e., the Holy Spirit). In the Greek language there are two words which get translated into English as "another." One is *heteros*. This means another of a different kind. "I'll give you another coin" can mean that I will give you a quarter to replace your dime. The other Greek word for "another" is *allos*. This means another of exactly the same kind. Jesus is implying that He has been a helper (*paracletos*, one called alongside to help) and now He will ask the Father to send another Helper exactly like Him. Then He says (verse 18), "I won't leave you as orphans, I will come to you." It could be that He is talking about coming to them after the resurrection. However, in the flow of the context of John 14, I believe He is saying, when the Spirit is here Jesus is here. One day I was having a dialogue with the Lord. As I was listening to Him speak to me, I said, "Excuse me, who am I talking to — the Father, the Son, or the Holy Spirit?" He said, "Yes."

One of my seminary professors said it this way: the Holy Spirit is the proxy-presence of Jesus. We know that a proxy is someone who stands in or is able to vote or carry out functions legally for another. This is the Holy Spirit. He is the proxy for Jesus, who is at the right hand of the Father (Acts 2:33; Heb. 1:3). By the way, since we have His Spirit in our spirit, we are His proxies on earth: we represent (re-present) Him!

THE PROMISE OF TEACHING AND REMEMBERING

<u>John 14:23</u> Jesus answered and said to him, " If anyone loves Me, he will keep My word; and My Father will love him, and We will come to him and make Our abode with him. 24 "He who does not love Me does not keep My words; and the word which you hear is not Mine, but the Father's who sent Me.

John 14:25 "These things I have spoken to you while abiding with you. 26 "But the Helper, the Holy Spirit, whom the Father will send in My name, He will teach you all things, and bring to your remembrance all that I said to you.

Jesus here provides us with another promise of the Spirit. Again the Spirit's teaching ministry is given but added this time is that the Spirit will bring to the disciples' remembrance all that Jesus had said to them. In other words, it is the Holy Spirit's job to remind us of things, the things Jesus said. Now we can quench this work of the Spirit; we can brush it off; we can be insensitive to this ministry. Our participation is required in the reception of these remembrances. There are times and situations in which the Lord wants to, by the Spirit working in our spirit, bring to our minds His word. In crucial times in our lives, when it will mean the most to us, He wants us to remember His word. Jesus promised the disciples in Matthew 10 that they would be dragged in front of courts on account of His name. He comforted them by saying in those situations the Spirit would teach them what to say (vv. 17-20).

This does not negate preparation or memorization of the Scripture. Those are well-proven spiritual disciplines. I see both dynamics at work in my teaching. I prepare for teaching and training times. I have notes most of the time that I work on ahead of time. Almost every time, however, as I am teaching, the Holy Spirit will bring to my mind other Scriptures or other spiritual truths that can amplify or apply what I am teaching.

I was trained in seminary to spend 20 hours of preparation for a 1 hour sermon. When one professor was asked how long to spend in preparation, replied, "Whatever it takes." So this was the way I was trained. I followed this routine for several years. However, in 1989 I was going to be at a conference all week long. I asked the Lord before I left town what I was supposed to teach on the next Sunday so I could start preparing. He said, "I will tell you what to say when you stand up to speak." I panicked! All week long at the conference I tried to think, to pray, to beg the Lord to give me some indication of the message. I was a nervous wreck! I received nothing. The following Sunday upon my return, I was standing during our singing time, still asking the Lord what/from which passage to teach – "Please, please tell me!" When the time arrived to stand and speak, I arose, and led the congregation in prayer. As I was beginning to close, the Lord spoke the passage to me out of the gospel of John. It was so vivid that I closed the prayer, "in John's name, Amen"! The Holy Spirit in that situation wanted to bring to my mind what to say. This happened often, but each time it does, it unravels me (less and less the more it happens!). The Lord was training me to depend upon the Spirit, not upon my education. There is nothing wrong with education; I love my education and I am thankful for it. But in that situation the Lord was saying, "Totally depend upon Me."

BEARING WITNESS

John 15:26 "When the Helper comes, whom I will send to you from the Father, that is the Spirit of truth who proceeds from the Father, He will testify about Me, 27 and you will testify also, because you have been with Me from the beginning.

The promised activity of the Holy Spirit here is that He will bear witness of Christ in us, first, and then through us ("and you will testify also"). The revelation of Jesus that we get isn't always just for us. In fact, most of the time that revelation isn't just for us. We receive a "testimony" of Jesus to pass on to those with whom we relate. Jesus said, " For I did not speak on My own initiative, but the Father Himself who sent Me has given Me a commandment as to what to say and what to speak (John 12:49). He "bore witness" of the Father. We bear witness of Him.

I am definitely not against apologetics, the art and knowledge of presenting Christ and our faith in an intelligent way. However, there are times in which the Spirit within us tells us what to say to those we are talking to, just the right things at the time. I don't have to come up with all the right arguments. I have a saying ..."If someone can be argued into the kingdom, they can be argued out." I know of several examples in which this has happened.

Coming into the kingdom must be an encounter. We come, as little children, to be birthed from above (see Jesus' "argument" in John 3 with Nicodemus).

John 16:7 "But I tell you the truth, it is to your advantage that I go away; for if I do not go away, the Helper will not come to you; but if I go, I will send Him to you. 8 "And He, when He comes, will convict the world concerning sin and righteousness and judgment; 9 concerning sin, because they do not believe in Me; 10 and concerning righteousness, because I go to the Father and you no longer see Me; 11 and concerning judgment, because the ruler of this world has been judged. 12 "I have many more things to say to you, but you cannot bear them now. 13 "But when He, the Spirit of truth, comes, He will guide you into all the truth; for He will not speak on His own initiative, but whatever He hears, He will speak; and He will disclose to you what is to come. 14 "He will glorify Me, for He will take of Mine and will disclose it to you. 15 " All things that the Father has are Mine; therefore I said that He takes of Mine and will disclose it to you.

Part of the Holy Spirit's job description is to "convict the world of sin, righteousness, and judgment." Dear friends, my wife, and I have been involved in a ministry for close to 15 years on the streets of Dallas, Texas. We have ministered in an area of town called "Deep Ellum" — a place of bars, tattoo parlors, psychic readers, and shops. When we first arrived in 1997 there were hundreds of people, mainly young people, on the streets on the weekends. We went to do "worship evangelism." In other words, we wanted to go down to the same location at the same time every week (11 p.m. to 1 a.m.) and worship on the streets the way we worshipped in our church building every Sunday morning. Initially, that's all we did. We took several guitars and djembe drums, set up, began to play, sing, and pray. We did not preach. We did not hand out any literature. We did not even start a conversation with anyone the first 3 Fridays we went. About the fourth Friday, some of the young people passing by would stop and say, "Who are you guys? Every time we have walked by here we feel different." Our main goal, initially, was to invite the presence of the Lord, the presence of the Holy Spirit, into that environment. When some of these young people walked into His presence, they were convicted of their sin (and, subsequently, became followers of Jesus). When the Holy Spirit is present, He convicts the world of sin, righteousness, and judgment!

Again, let me emphasize that I am not "against" evangelism. We do need to present the good news of the kingdom. Romans 10 (vv. 14-15)is clear of the process: being sent, preaching, hearing, calling upon Him. I believe that salvation is a process, slow or fast. There is a preparation time during which many people, perhaps, are involved in someone's life as "planting seeds." There comes a time, an experience, a testimony — whatever or whomever the Lord uses — in which those seeds bring forth fruit. But in each and every case we must believe that the "conversion" of that precious human being is dependent upon the work of the Holy Spirit and not upon how convincing I can be.

GUIDING INTO ALL THE TRUTH

The other job description of the Holy Spirit in this passage is to "guide you into all the truth." Many times when I am having trouble grasping the understanding of a Biblical passage, I will pray, "Holy Spirit, guide me into the truth; guide me into the truth."

THE COMING OF POWER

<u>Luke 24:49</u> "And behold, I am sending forth the promise of My Father upon you; but you are to stay in the city until you are clothed with power from on high."

Jesus equates the coming of the Holy Spirit (when He descended upon the church in Acts 2) with the coming of empowerment. If the Holy Spirit is truly present, then sooner or later there must be an evidence of power. It may be power over sin. It may be power over disease; it may be power over the work of the enemy (satan). It may be power to overcome temptation to sin. It may be power to resist depression. This power may manifest itself in a myriad of ways. But if the Spirit is present, power will be seen. If there is no evidence of power in a believer's life, then there is a clear need for a change to take place. There is a lid over the "container" (our spirit), holding in the activity of the Holy Spirit. And the lid needs to be removed. Paul says, "for the kingdom of God does not consist in words but in power" (1 Cor. 4:20). I have lived too much of my Christian life based upon "words" and not upon "power." Honestly, it comes to a point where we must say "put up or shut up"! If this God of ours is real, then He must demonstrate Himself. We have a part to play in our openness to the Spirit working within and through us. We have a part to play in the exercise of our faith. But our faith must be real. The world must know that our God is real and active and powerful.

I know there is a danger of getting "power crazy" or "power focused". We must maintain our focus and desire for the Lord Himself. We must welcome and steward the presence of the Lord. But if He is present we will see power (as well as so many other of His wonderful attributes). I love the way I have seen this balance worked out at Bethel Church in Redding, California. Bethel has seen sustained revival (not revival that comes and goes or comes for a short time) for 17 years. They have found ways to cultivate a "habitation" for the Lord. And in that environment works of power take place. A friend who has spent 3 years there told me that he either experienced or heard of miraculous works every single day he was there. I believe this is a model, especially for the American church. This is taking place regularly in churches in other parts of the world.

I believe that one of the enemy's chief strategies against Christians is to cause us to believe we have little or no power. If he (and the deceptive activity of his demons) can get us to believe that, to disregard the authority we have been delegated as sons and daughters of God who have "resident power" (the life of Jesus the risen Christ) in us, then we are no threat to him.

<u>Acts 1:8</u> "but you will receive power when the Holy Spirit has come upon you; and you shall be My witnesses both in Jerusalem, and in all Judea and Samaria, and even to the remotest part of the earth."

Again, Jesus promises the coming of the Holy Spirit with power. This time He speaks of power to witness. We see this working out in the remainder of the book of Acts. Peter, Stephen, Philip, Paul and others powerfully witness to the death, burial, and resurrection of Jesus. But with these powerful declarations are also powerful demonstrations of the Spirit. Much the same is seen in the prior "missionary mission" of the 12 and the 70 (Luke 9 and 10) who were sent by our Lord to preach the kingdom but also to heal and cast out demons. Declaration must be accompanied by demonstration. Sometimes Jesus demonstrated the kingdom first, got the attention of His audience, and then declared the truths of the reign of the Father. These are the "works" we have already seen promised by Jesus to those who believe in John 14.

THE HOLY SPIRIT COMES

Prior to the descent of the Spirit in Acts 2 the congregation of believers were praying for Him to come. In Acts 1:14 we see their activity: "These all with one mind were continually devoting themselves to (Literally, in the Greek) THE prayer,..." What was THE prayer? I believe it was the prayer for the promised Holy Spirit: "Holy Spirit, come!"

In chapter 2 of Acts, it happened.

<u>Acts 2:1</u> When the day of Pentecost had come, they were all together in one place. 2 And suddenly there came from heaven a noise like a violent rushing wind, and it filled the whole house where they were sitting. 3 And there appeared to them tongues as of fire distributing themselves, and they rested on each one of them. 4 And they were all filled with the Holy Spirit and began to speak with other tongues, as the Spirit was giving them utterance.

Luke, the author of Acts, uses a number of terms to describe this experience of the Holy Spirit. Jesus says that His followers will be "baptized" (1:5). He also says that the Holy Spirit will "come upon" them (1:8). In 2:4 Luke writes that at the coming of the Spirit the believers were "filled." Peter, in his sermon refers to this experience as a fulfillment of Joel's prophecy that uses the terminology of the Spirit being "poured out" (2:17-18; see also the experience of Cornelius and his household, 10:45). Peter, at the end of the sermon tells his listeners to "receive" the Spirit (2:38). Simon, the former magic practitioner, sees that the Spirit was "received" by the laying on of the apostles' hands (8:17). When Peter describes the experience of Cornelius and his household to believers in Jerusalem as the Spirit "fell upon" them and equated it with the promised "baptism" promised by the Lord (11:16-17).

What's my point? My point is that, I believe, Luke isn't as precise in his terminology as we want to be with this experience. Baptized, coming upon, filled, poured out, received, falling upon all describe the same thing. The importance is that it was an experience. I believe that these people knew and saw and believed and experienced the Holy Spirit.

We fight over terminology about a "second baptism" of the Spirit. I believe there is a second baptism ... and a third ... and a forty-second ... and so on. The basic meaning of the word "baptize" in Greek, *baptizo*, means to be overwhelmed. So, rather than get into an argument over terminology, let me ask you, "Have you ever been OVERWHELMED by the Holy Spirit?" Even Peter, who was "filled" in chapter 2 gets re-filled twice in chapter 4 (vv. 8 and 31). We need to be repeatedly filled, baptized, and overwhelmed with the Spirit (Eph. 5:18, "be being filled with the Spirit").

In so many of these "experiences" with the Holy Spirit in the book of Acts, those who were present "saw" something. There were evidences like tongues of fire, speaking in tongues, boldness in preaching the gospel, and a house shaking. In the instances referred to above, Simon in Acts 8 and those present at Cornelius' house, the Scriptures say Simon and those present "saw" the Holy Spirit being given. They SAW something. There was an observable phenomenon of the presence of the Spirit's work.

In light of all this, if a person comes to me and asks me if I am "Spirit-filled", I must answer, "Wait a minute, let me check." What they might seem to imply is have I been "baptized" in the Spirit with some evidence. What the New Testament means by a "Spirit-filled" believer is: I am presently being controlled by the Spirit. Is the Spirit ruling in my life right now?

My understanding is that we who have genuinely believed in Jesus, who have accepted His work on the cross, and who have exchanged our life for His, are given the Holy Spirit (see Romans 8:9 among many other N.T. locations). The Spirit comes to reside in our spirit like a great river of living water (John 7:37-39). But like an underground stream, it seeks a way out. The Spirit wants to overwhelm me, affect my thinking, affect my decisions, affect and direct my feelings, and even affect me physically. The Spirit is like the Old Faithful geyser in Yellowstone intended to regularly spring up and overwhelm us.

Now I lived the first sixteen years of my Christian life believing that God only spoke through the Bible. During that time did I have "experiences" with the Holy Spirit? Yes, I did. The Holy Spirit worked in and through me on many occasions. But there came a day in 1985 when I was "overwhelmed." I do not believe that the experience I had was the Holy Spirit coming "upon" me from the outside. I believe, since I already had the Holy Spirit, He "gushed up" from within me.

A little Greek grammar to make a point: In Acts 2, Peter, among the 120 believers in the upper room, was "filled with the Holy Spirit." In Greek grammar, there are tenses that are a little more specific than in English grammar. In English we have, basically, past, present, and future tense. In Greek there is a tense called the aorist tense. When a writer (in this case Luke writing Acts) uses the aorist tense he is saying the action (verb) took place at a particular time in the past. It happened in the past but it happened right then. If the writer had wanted us to know that the action took place in the past but kept happening, he would have used a different tense. So, here in Acts 2:4, Peter (with the others) was filled with the Holy Spirit right then and there. Later, in Acts 4:8, as Peter and John are before the Jewish leaders, Luke says that Peter "was filled with the Holy Spirit" (again, in the aorist tense). The same occurrence happened to Paul in Acts 9:17 and again in Acts 13:9. What's my point? For both Peter and Paul (and for us) they were filled with the Spirit on one occasion but needed or were filled with the Spirit on another occasion. It happens over and over again. This is why Ephesians 5:18 says "be (being) filled with the Spirit" (continual action). We need to be filled over and over and over again with the Spirit. It is necessary that we be filled (and controlled) by the Spirit on a continual basis. In any situation the question will be whether my emotions (or thinking or my own will) will be in control or whether the Holy Spirit (working in my spirit) will be in control.

The kingdom of God is about a rule; it's about a reign. Will we allow God to be king, to rule in our lives? Where? Initially, in our spirit and, ultimately, in our whole being. How? By the Holy Spirit. Many times as we confront problems in our lives, we try to fix our problems by "soulish" means. We will try to think something out or consider how we feel about something. But we will never even ask the Spirit! We might throw up a prayer. But as we will see later, we need to cultivate a sensitivity to the work of the Spirit in our spirit that gives us direction.

The Holy Spirit, having been given to those who put their faith and trust in Jesus, now has a ministry in our lives.

POURING OUT THE FATHER'S LOVE

Rom. 5:1 Therefore, having been justified by faith, we have peace with God through our Lord Jesus Christ, 2 through whom also we have obtained our introduction by faith into this grace in which we stand; and we exult in hope of the glory of God. 3 And not only this, but we also exult in our tribulations, knowing that tribulation brings about perseverance; 4 and perseverance, proven character; and proven character, hope; 5 and hope does not disappoint, because the love of God has been poured out within our hearts through the Holy Spirit who was given to us.

Paul's great treatise on the work of God to bring us to himself here focuses upon the justification (a legal term, to have a penalty taken care of) by the faith we exercise in coming to Jesus. This justification is for a purpose: to have peace with (to be reconciled in relationship with) God. If you ask most Christians, "Why did Jesus come to earth?" the answer usually sounds like "to save us from our sins." Jesus' substitutionary death on the cross as a payment for our sins was only a means to an end. The end purpose/result of the cross is to bring us to, to reunite us to our Father (see 2 Cor. 5:18-19; 1 Pet. 3:18). This moves God's work from a legal action into a relational action. He doesn't just want to get us out of jail. He wants to have a relationship with us. We are not to have a relationship with God as a judge, nor as an attorney (He acts as both). We are to have a relationship with God as our Father.

Having done this, we "stand in grace." The way I picture this is that grace is an environment, a "room" if you will, in which we stand. In this room or environment of grace a process is taking place that starts with finding a different perspective from which to view life. Therefore we can rejoice even in the tough stuff because we know that we are in the process of maturity. This process (indicated here in Romans 5) ends in hope. I define biblical hope (as contrasted to the world's definition of hope: something I wish for) as "the absolute confidence that what God has promised He will faithfully fulfill." How do we know that God will faithfully fulfill His promises? The activity of the Holy Spirit in our lives shows us. Primarily, this activity is the "pouring out" of God's love in our hearts. God promised the Holy Spirit to those who believe. Every time we experience God's love in its many forms it is a reminder that God keeps His promises.

As I said above, if the Holy Spirit lives within our spirit, and a filling (or gushing forth) takes place, one purpose of that filling is to let us know and experience the love of God. Most of us, however, try to experience the love of God in our soul. Or we try to "understand" the love of God. We try, initially, to "feel" the love of God. Both of these dynamics – understanding and feeling - may take place. But the origin of the love is in our spirit. I have had times when I've walked around feeling, physically and emotionally, the love of God. That feeling (my emotions) has been affected by the work of the Spirit flowing out of my spirit.

The Challenge of Romans 8

As we begin to look at the work of the Spirit in our spirit in Romans 8 let me deliver a challenge. The book of Romans, as far as we know and have the earliest manuscripts, was written in Greek. In the epistle (letter) form, the Greek was written, letter next to letter and without capitalization. What the translators and editors of our English bibles have done is to make a decision for us. They have divided the words and put capitalization on words. The Greek word for "spirit" is pneuma. This word occurs 21 times in Romans 8. Many of these times, in the context of the passage, "pneuma" refers to the Spirit of God. A few times, it is clear that "pneuma" refers to our human spirit. My challenge, however, is for you to go through chapter 8 and make every capital "S" on Spirit a lower-case s. Then go back through and read the chapter again. Obviously, you will have to replace some of the lower case "s's" with a capital, as I said above. But my point is that I believe Paul wants us to see the activity of our spirit in a greater way than the editors of our English versions.

Setting Our Minds

<u>Romans 8:5</u> For those who are according to the flesh set their minds on the things of the flesh, but those who are according to the Spirit, the things of the Spirit.

Another of the job descriptions of the Spirit in our spirit is to help us "set our minds on the things of the Spirit (or spirit)." What does that look like? The Holy Spirit moves within us to cause us to desire to think about, concentrate on, and give attention to the things (the words, the activities, the perspective) of the Spirit. I WANT to see things from God's point of view.

In a similar way: Phil. 2:12 So then, my beloved, just as you have always obeyed, not as in my presence only, but now much more in my absence, work out your salvation with fear and trembling; 13 for it is God who is at work in you, both to will and to work for His good pleasure. God is at work in us (by the Spirit) to WILL (create the desire) and to WORK (give us the wherewithal to carry out) His good pleasure. That's the Holy Spirit's job. Rom. 8:9 However, you are not in the flesh but in the Spirit, if indeed the Spirit of God dwells in you. But if anyone does not have the Spirit of Christ, he does not belong to Him.

You are "in the Spirit" if the Spirit is "in you." The presence of the Spirit in our spirit is a certainty if we know Jesus. The issue is whether we will yield and let Him out.

Putting To Death The Deeds of the Body

Romans 8:13 for if you are living according to the flesh, you must die; but if by the Spirit you are putting to death the deeds of the body, you will live. 14 For all who are being led by the Spirit of God, these are sons of God. 15 For you have not received a spirit of slavery leading to fear again, but you have received a spirit of adoption as sons by which we cry out, " Abba! Father!" 16 The Spirit Himself testifies with our spirit that we are children of God, 17 and if children, heirs also, heirs of God and fellow heirs with Christ, if indeed we suffer with Him so that we may also be glorified with Him.
A number of activities of the Spirit within us are listed here. The first is that we can, by the Spirit, put to death the deeds of the body. How do we do that? How does that happen? How does that work?

There is a natural principle as well as a spiritual principle. The principle is: what you feed, grows. What you do not feed, starves to death. Are we feeding the spirit or the flesh? If we feed on truth, the spirit grows in truth. If we feed ourselves lies, that's what's going to grow. "Put to death" means to hold a funeral for the things we have been hooked on, cravings, destructive attitudes and practices.

This story is in another of my books (<u>Kingdom Come! Tales of the Supernatural God</u>): my wife and I and another couple were in a hotel room praying for a friend. By a vision given to one of us, it was shown that this woman was having a lesbian relationship with another woman in our church. When this vision was shared with the woman and she was asked about it in a loving way, she admitted to the relationship. We asked her, "Are you willing for this relationship to die, today, not just to get away from the relationship but for the relationship to die? This will mean that the relationship is over; it's buried; it's gone." She was ready for this to happen. As we then began to pray for her, she began to wail — a mourning wail. She was mourning a death. But the relationship was over.

That's what the Spirit in our spirit does. He enables us to have a funeral.

The Leading Of The Spirit

Verse 14: "for all who are being led by the Spirit of God, these are the sons of God."

The Holy Spirit is to lead us, to guide us. I have pointed out already the imperative in Galatians 5:25: "If we live by the Spirit, let us also walk by the Spirit." The word "walk" here is a military term. It means to keep in step, rank and file, with the Spirit. In order to be led by the Spirit we must be close to the Spirit. And we must be encouraged by the truth that the Spirit wants to lead us.

To Testify That We Are God's Children

Verse 16: "The Spirit Himself testifies with our spirit that we are children of God."

And before verse 16 in verse 15 it tells us that the Spirit initiates the cry of "Abba, Father." "Abba" was the Hebrew term that small children called their father. "Daddy" is an equivalent. The Spirit moves us to cry out to our Father in a childlike, intimate way, "Daddy!" The Spirit reminds us and cements in our deepest place of conviction that we are His kids. If a believer is having a hard time believing, sensing, or feeling their sonship with God, something is blocking the work of the Holy Spirit.

Hebrews 12 says, "7 It is for discipline that you endure; God deals with you as with sons; for what son is there whom his father does not discipline? 8 But if you are without discipline, of which all have become partakers, then you are illegitimate children and not sons." What this is telling us is that if we are sons we will be disciplined. And one of the things that blocks this sonship-affirming work of the Spirit is our rebellion, our resistance to the discipline of our Father. This is one of the major ways God shows His love toward us and if we keep resisting and resisting and stiff-arming His discipline, at some point we will not believe, sense, or feel the love of the Father.

The Holy Spirit is constantly saying, "You're God child. You are His son. You are his daughter." I get up every day believing that I'm our Father's favorite son. And you can too (I remind women that they are female sons, just like men are part of the bride of Christ). I believe that I will walk through each day with God's favor resting upon me because I am a favorite son. It doesn't mean that I sail smoothly through each day without difficulties. But it does mean that I approach life differently. I see things differently. That's so much different than getting up every day believing and saying "I'm just a sinner. I just barely got in. As the garage door of heaven was coming down, I just slid in. I'm going to walk around today with God just waiting for me to step just an inch out of line. And I'm going to get smacked." See the difference? I am looking, every day, for the goodness of God.

This is also one of the purposes of the spiritual gift of prophecy. The purpose of prophecy in I Corinthians 14 is that it brings "exhortation, edification, and comfort." Prophecy can speak to me and exhort me and/or edify (strengthen) me and/or comfort me to believe and live out of who God says I am. God may speak (and I have witnessed this over and over and over again) to people to tell them what He thinks of them, to affirm His love and their sonship, to pull them out of a perverted, mixed up concept of themselves.

Interceding

<u>Rom. 8:26</u> In the same way the Spirit also helps our weakness; for we do not know how to pray as we should, but the Spirit Himself intercedes for us with groanings too deep for words;

The Spirit helps us pray. In the next verse (27) it tells us that the reason the Spirit can do this is because He knows the mind of God. So the Spirit is within me (in my spirit) praying and interceding. I may be mentally connected with that. I may not be connected. I do not believe that this verse is specifically talking about praying in tongues (I Cor. 14:3). That is one possibility. But the Spirit is praying in me and through me and maybe I understand that prayer in my mind and maybe I don't. I just have the confidence that if I am praying something, that as it rises to the throne of God, the Spirit may "untwist" my prayer and say, "This is what he really means, Father." The Spirit knows my heart.

I've learned a lot about prayer by raising 3 children. When my children were little sometimes they would come to me with requests. They wanted this thing or that. Knowing their heart, many times I would give them what they needed, not what they wanted. Sometimes I would give them what they wanted, knowing it wasn't that good for them but that a lesson would be learned. And sometimes I would give them gifts without them asking (not on their birthdays or on Christmas). Why? Just because I loved them. Our heavenly Father responds to our requests in the same way.

Our verse here says that the Spirit prays "with groanings too deep for words." The word "groaning" (Greek, *stenagmos*) occurs in Mark 7:34: and looking up to heaven with a deep sigh, He (Jesus) said to him, "*Ephphatha!*" that is, "Be opened!" What is happening here? Jesus, who relied upon the Holy Spirit entirely, is being moved, with a groan, to "pray" to heaven concerning the healing of the deaf-mute. The Holy Spirit was working in Jesus, giving us an example, of His intercessory ministry. I, and others, have had this experience. I am aware that something is going on deep, deep inside me. I cannot put words on it, but I know something is taking place in my spirit. All I can do is groan. All I can do it look to heaven and groan. Often, when this happens, all

I know is that there is something "wrong" that needs to be "right." And all I can do is groan. When we say, "Let's pray" we think of words. Here, we see an example of prayer without words. One of the entries in Strong's Greek Concordance for this word is "to pray inaudibly." One lady liken this kind of praying to giving birth to her daughter. As the birth was taking place, she groaned uncontrollably. This type of prayer is giving birth; it's delivering something that is deep within us out and up to God.

In referring to all these activities of the Holy Spirit within me, within my spirit, my point is to get us to start thinking, "How does this work? How does the Spirit want to work in me in this way? What does this look like? How can I participate with the Spirit to see these activities in my life?"

Sometimes I've prayed (in English words) all I've known to pray. Sometimes I just don't know what else to pray. In those situations I try to get quiet and get "in touch" with the Holy Spirit within me. Then, much of the time, He will either give me words or tongues or just a sighing or groaning "too deep for words." These are opportunities to submit to the Holy Spirit's control.

Boiling in Spirit

Romans 12:11 not lagging behind in diligence, fervent in spirit, serving the Lord;

We "plop down" in this verse in the middle of Paul's list of characteristics of a loving community of people living in the reality of the kingdom of God. "Fervent in spirit" means that our spirit is to be boiling, bubbling! What does a boiling spirit look like? We have differing personalities. But whether we tend to be a sanguine, out-going person or a choleric, staid, intense person we are all to have a "boiling" spirit. Again, we Christians read over these verses and keep going without thinking about what this should look like in my life. To be boiling looks like (as the mental picture implies) a solid or liquid turning to gas. There is change taking place. It is expansive; there is more movement and action. The activity of the Holy Spirit within me is "bigger" and more effective in my life. A fervent spirit will be more sensitive to things spiritually. Just like our expanding gas picture, a fervent spirit seeks an outlet (or it will explode). This is why, in this verse, the next kingdom operation is "serving the Lord." A fervent spirit seeks to serve.

As the fervent spirit seeks an outlet, the Lord provides ways to serve Him– "in praying for others, in giving time, energy, attention, and money, and in worshipping Him.

As was pointed out to me, different liquids boil differently. Whatever is "inside" us, as the heating process begins, will be brought to the surface. As a soup or stew is beginning to boil on a range top, the aroma of the ingredients begins to fill the house. Many times the boiling of our spirit is to raise the impurities of our lives to the surface so that they can be removed and the wonderful aroma of a pure, Holy Spirit-filled spirit may waft through the air to everyone around. Have you ever entered someone's house and immediate begin to smell something cooking? You say, "What's that you're cooking? What is that?" As our spirits boil, the aroma ought to be attractive: 2 Cor. 2:15 For we are a fragrance of Christ to God among those who are being saved and among those who are perishing; 16 to the one an aroma from death to death, to the other an aroma from life to life.

Source of Righteousness, Peace and Joy

Romans 14:17 for the kingdom of God is not eating and drinking, but righteousness and peace and joy in the Holy Spirit.

The kingdom of God is the rule or reign of a loving Father in our lives. Here it says that the kingdom "is" (or is equal to or is expressed by) righteousness, peace and joy in the Holy Spirit. If righteousness, peace and joy are found in the Spirit, then He is the One to whom I go to receive them. I am not setting up a set of rules to be right or live righteously. I am not setting up some "soulish" procedures to get peaceful. I am not counting on circumstances going my way to have joy. What I do is go to the "place" where I receive these things – the Holy Spirit living within my spirit. I know that I have, often, tried to go "outside" somewhere to get righteousness, peace and joy. I've tried to get them from situations, locations, and people. I try to gain righteousness from doing my "check list" of Christian things to do. I try to get peace from listening to worship music (NOTE: I am not against worship music. I listen almost every day!). But the music itself or the activity of having worship music playing doesn't guarantee peace. If my faith or dependence is in the music rather than in Him, I've gone to the wrong source. Can the Lord use worship music? Absolutely. But my point is, where does the interaction take place? Am I interacting with the person of God, with His Spirit?

Overflow with Hope

Romans 15:13 Now may the God of hope fill you with all joy and peace in believing, so that you will abound in hope by the power of the Holy Spirit.

The Holy Spirit is the source of our hope. Remember my definition of hope – the absolute certainty that what God has promised He will fulfill. The Lord desires that we overflow with this certainty. "Now faith is the assurance of things hoped for,…" Faith is connected to hope. If I am certain about my Father's promises I can walk in faith. Hope is connected to God's promises. So it is the Holy Spirit's job to remind my of those promises. As I am reminded and put my faith in those promises, it expands. There are a lot of things we Christians should be "leaking." One of those is hope. In Romans 5 we are reminded that hope is apparent when we are in afflictions. How we go through the afflictions of life can attract the attention of others. In the midst of being afflicted, if we are walking around leaking hope (abounding in hope) some people may come to us and say, "How are you doing this? I don't understand." Then we have an opportunity to "make a defense to everyone who asks you to give an account for the hope that is in you" (1 Pet. 3:15).

Sanctifying Work

Romans 15:16 to be a minister of Christ Jesus to the Gentiles, ministering as a priest the gospel of God, so that my offering of the Gentiles may become acceptable, sanctified by the Holy Spirit.

The Holy Spirit sanctifies us. To sanctify means to set apart for holy use. To be sanctified by the Holy Spirit means that He is working in us to make us holy. We can depend upon the Spirit, speaking and working in our spirit, to touch and point out areas of our life that need God's purification or need God's control. I cannot tell you how many times, as I have become convinced of the sanctifying work of the Spirit, instead of me having to go confront someone about sin, I just pray. I ask the Spirit to work a sanctifying work in their lives. And, often, it works! They will come to me and say, "The Lord has really convicted me about _____." I don't have to say a word. Sometimes I still do have to speak with people. But even with these folks I believe that the Spirit has already been trying to speak to them about their issue(s).

A number of years ago a young couple began attending our church. They were living together, not married. After a few weeks we leaders were speaking and praying together (on a Monday night) about who should go talk with them and urge them to separate or prepare for a godly marriage, and be wed. The next day one of the our leaders was approached by this young man. He told him that the night before (while we were praying) the Lord had led him to tell the young lady that what they were doing was not pleasing to the Lord, that he was moving out until they were ready to get married. The Holy Spirit was performing His sanctifying work. Now sometimes the Spirit uses us in these situations. But how about praying first? How about starting there, asking the Spirit to work? It is not our job to sanctify others; it is the Holy Spirit's job to sanctify them.

Power

Romans 15:18 For I will not presume to speak of anything except what Christ has accomplished through me, resulting in the obedience of the Gentiles by word and deed, 19 in the power of signs and wonders, in the power of the Spirit; so that from Jerusalem and round about as far as Illyricum I have fully preached the gospel of Christ.

Paul is describing his ministry. In doing so he parallels the power of signs and wonders with the power of the Spirit.

This stirs up something that leads me to mount a soapbox. Paul says in 1 Corinthians 4: 20: For the kingdom of God does not consist in words but in power. The kingdom doesn't consist in words. It consists in power. Most of my Christian life has been about words—words, words, words, words from books, words from sermons, words from tapes and recorded messages, words, words, words. The world will not be reached or changed with words. The kingdom of this world, the domain of darkness, will not be overcome with words. A power encounter requires power. We followers of Jesus must take demonstrations (power) of the kingdom with us wherever we go. Our words will mean little or nothing alone. I believe that every follower of Jesus can walk in power: power for signs and wonders (healings, deliverances, salvations, miracles), power to forgive, power over temptations, and power to overcome the work of the our enemy. We have the life of Jesus within us ... resident power. Paul prays that we know the "surpassing greatness of His power toward us who believe" (Eph. 1:19).

Many times we see the terms "signs and wonders" and we think of the dramatic miracles and healings. Often, biblically, this is true. Yet what is a "sign"? A sign is a pointer — it points to something else. What is a "wonder"? It is whatever inspires awe. Our lives, just as we live them under the rule of God, can be signs and wonders. The supernatural way in which we live our lives can be signs that point to the reality of the God who lives in us. The way in which we live can inspire awe in those who see us and/or know us. In any case, the Holy Spirit lives within us to release power for living.
Paul mentions that he has "fully preached the gospel." Now, he may be referring to the fact that he has gone everywhere the Lord wanted him to go (Jerusalem to Illyricum). Could it mean that fully preaching the gospel is through signs and wonders and in the power of the Spirit? I am living out

a purpose that I believe the Lord has given me. I want to "kingdomize" everyone I meet. I want believers to believe that they can walk in signs and wonders. I want them to begin to risk stepping out and trust the Lord to use them powerfully in their spheres of influence. I had lunch recently with a new friend. He has spent three years at Bethel Church in Redding, California. I asked him what that was like. He said that in that environment miracles happen every day. He said he was there for about three months before he began to believe he could be involved in seeing miracles take place. Then he stepped out and they began to happen. It requires a stepping out — an exercise of faith and taking the opportunities Father gives us to minister to others.

Recently I had lunch with another man who, years ago, was in the Philippines with Youth With A Mission. He told me they had been going from village to village praying for the sick. He said that they had not seen anyone immediately healed. Perhaps some had been healed after they left, but they had not personally witnessed any healing. On a following day the group was asked to come to another village and pray for a woman who had been unable to walk for 26 years. My friend went, not believing that anything would take place. He walked into the hut thinking he would lay hands on this woman, pray for healing, and walk out. He told me, "John, I had no faith that this woman would be healed. Even as I was praying, I was thinking about walking out." But the woman immediately arose and began to walk. She told them, through the translator, "I knew when you walked in my door, I was going to be healed." If you asked this man if he has the gift of healing he would say no. But there was a sign and a wonder demonstrated through him. It could be through you tomorrow, or next week. You might not have the gift of healing or the gift of prophecy. But you might prophesy one time in your life and completely change the person's life who receives it. You may pray for 200 people to be healed and one person gets healed. But think about that one person. My percentage of people getting healed went up when I started praying for people to get healed! In the first 16 years of my walk with Christ, I prayed for no one to receive healing. I prayed for the doctors to have wisdom and to heal them and for the patients to be comforted. Guess what? In the last 27 years when I have prayed for healing I have witnessed the Lord heal many. That, to me, is the gospel, the good news — that Jesus saves AND Jesus heals.

Eph. 5:18 And do not get drunk with wine, for that is dissipation, but be filled with the Spirit, 19 speaking to one another in psalms and hymns and spiritual songs, singing and making melody with your heart to the Lord; 20 always giving thanks for all things in the name of our Lord Jesus Christ to God, even the Father; 21 and be subject to one another in the fear of Christ.

The Greek in this verse can be translated "be being filled." Being filled means we are not the ones filling ourselves, someone else is doing this for me or to me. "Be being" filled means continuous. I (we) need to be filled over and over and over again, constantly. What follows are evidences that we are filled – speaking, singing and making melody, giving thanks, and being subject. When someone says they are "Spirit-filled" I may ask, "How are you about submitting to others?" That is one of the tell-tale signs that a person is filled with the Spirit.

What if a group of people really lived this way? I believe it would change the world. In the first century this is the way the church was living. And it permeated the Roman empire. Today, in many places (many places where the church is being persecuted), Christians are living this way and impacting their families, friends, and neighbors.

My wife and I have been graced to experience many, many things of the Lord's presence and power. My book, <u>Kingdom Come! Tales of the Supernatural God</u>, chronicles several of these supernatural experiences. We are so thankful for these. But I want more, just like Paul wanted more. In the letter to the Philippians Paul is writing from his imprisonment in Rome. Therefore this is toward the end of his life. Paul, at this point, had been an apostle for almost 30 years. He had seen many signs and wonders. He had seen everyone on Malta who was sick healed (Acts 28:8-9). He had had visitations from the Lord Jesus Himself. In spite of all of this Paul wanted more: "that I may know Him and the power of His resurrection and the fellowship of His sufferings, being conformed to His death; in order that I may attain to the resurrection from the dead. Not that I have already obtained it or have already become perfect, but I press on so that I may lay hold of that for which also I was laid hold of by Christ Jesus. Brethren, I do not regard myself as having laid hold of it yet; but one thing I do: forgetting what lies behind and reaching forward to what lies ahead, I press on toward the goal for the prize of the upward call of God in Christ Jesus" (Phil. 3:10-14). Paul was certainly (even in the context of Philippians 3 earlier) thankful for all the Lord had done in his life. Yet he wanted more. So do I.

What The Holy Spirit Brings

When the Holy Spirit comes to indwell, to live within us (1 Cor. 3:16; 2 Tim. 1:14), what does He bring with Him?

He brings the fruit of the Spirit: "But the fruit of the Spirit is love, joy, peace, patience, kindness, goodness, faithfulness, gentleness, self-control; against such things there is no law"

(Galatians 5:22-23).
He brings us a greater spiritual awareness of the things of God (1 Cor. 2:10-12). He brings us a greater spiritual awareness of our spiritual nature.

He brings light. We have this "treasure" in our earthen vessels (our bodies). What treasure is that? 2 Corinthians tells us it is "the light of the knowledge of the glory of God in the face of Christ" (4:6-7). This light shines in the darkness in our own lives to expose what Father wants to transform in us. This light shines in the darkness of the domain of darkness all around us.

Since our God is a trinity — Father, Son and Spirit — the Holy Spirit connects us to all three.

He brings the gifts (Greek word, *charismata*) of the Spirit. In 1 Corinthians 1 Paul thanks God that this church is not lacking in any gift (v. 7). In other words, if we could have gone to Corinth in that day and looked at all the believers with the gifts God had given them, we would have to say that they had everything they needed. I believe that is our Lord's intention for every church today. The gifts of the Spirit are listed in various places in the New Testament. Since some "lists" include gifts that other lists don't (i.e. 1 Corinthians 12 speaks of the gifts of words of knowledge and words of wisdom which the other lists don't; Romans 12 speaks of the gift of leadership/ruling that other lists don't), I believe, therefore, that none of the lists are complete.

In Ephesians 4 our God wants to communicate to us that He has given us gifted *people*: apostles, prophets, evangelists, pastors and teachers (the Greek word for gifts in this passage is *doma* = a present). In the passage it says that these gifted people are to equip believers to do the work of ministry. This process of equipping is to continue until the body of Christ matures to reach the stature of Jesus. Has that happened yet? Are we, the church, the body of Christ, looking just like Jesus? Don't think so. Have we attained the unity of the faith? Don't think so. Therefore, this process and those needed for the process are still needed.

When the Holy Spirit comes, He brings all these things to believers and to the church. I want it all. For instance, in 1 Corinthians 12:31 and again in 14:1 Paul urges the Corinthians (which he has already said have every gift) to "desire spiritual gifts." What can that mean except that he wants them to desire all the gifts they have been given to function. He wants them to use the gifts they've been given. He wants them to experience all the Spirit brought to them. So do I.

On several occasions those wanting prayer for something have approached me. Often, I will direct them to others in the body by saying, "You know, so-and-so has seen dramatic results in praying for what you are asking me. Why don't you go ask them to pray?" What am I doing? I am encouraging more parts of the body to function in giftings the Lord has given them.

When the Holy Spirit comes, He brings power (Luke 24:49; Acts 1:8). One more aspect of the power-giving ministry of the Spirit is Paul's prayer for the Ephesians that they would be "strengthened with power through His Spirit in the inner man" (3:16).

When the Holy Spirit comes, He brings us the mind of Christ (1 Cor. 2:16). So, if I am trying to make a decision or figure something, I have the resource — the mind of Jesus. I can think like Jesus thought. If I can "get in touch" with His mind, I can use His wisdom. This doesn't mean I can shun or disregard others, their wisdom and counsel. But I must believe I have this resource living within me.

When the Holy Spirit comes, He brings worship. He brings worship because one of His jobs is to glorify Jesus (John 16:14) and to work from our spirit so that we may worship God "in spirit and in truth" (John 4:24).

When the Holy Spirit comes, He directs our prayers (Romans 8:26; Jude 20). Many times, when I am praying and I have prayed all I know to pray, I will stop and wait and listen in my spirit. Then I will begin to pray again; this time (I trust) praying prayers directed by the Spirit.

When the Holy Spirit comes, He brings encouragement. The word describing Him that Jesus uses several times, "Helper", literally in the Greek language means "one called alongside to encourage" (John 14:16, 26; 15:26; 16:7). This encouragement may take the form of exhortation (challenging us to live like who we are) or the form of comfort.

When the Holy Spirit comes, He brings guidance and direction. Listen to this prayer Paul prays for the church in Thessalonica: "May the Lord direct your hearts into the love of God and into the steadfastness of Christ. (2 Thess. 3:5)" I believe that all three members of the trinity are mentioned here and it is the Holy Spirit who is doing the directing (steering) of our hearts into the love of the Father and the steadfastness of the Son.

Recently, I was having lunch with a friend of mine at a local restaurant. I always ask the Lord if He wants me to communicate anything to a waiter or waitress. A young girl in her twenties was waiting our table. I felt that the Lord had given me some revelation for her. So when she brought us the check, I said to her, "I'm getting ready to say something to you that may seem really weird. You're going to be able to go home to your friends tonight and tell them what a weird customer you had today. But, sometimes I talk to God and sometimes He talks to me. Sometimes He talks to me about people that I'm with. I believe that He has told me something about you. I believe that He has told me that there was a desire, a vocational desire, in your heart and something stopped it." Before I said another word she started weeping. "And," I said, "the Lord says, 'Go for it! Now is the time to go for it!'" The young waitress, through her sniffles, said, "I've got to take these other customers their check. But please don't leave until I come back and tell you something." After she returned she knelt down by our table and said, "Last night I stayed awake all night because I was crying out to God. In 2008 I dedicated my life to do children's work and I walked away from it. Last night I was crying out to the Lord and saying, 'Lord, somehow You need to encourage me to get back into the ministry.'" That encounter was the release of rivers of living water! Guidance, direction, and answers to prayer!

In this instance, the Lord did not give me all of the information about this young lady ahead of time. I knew I was to communicate something, so I just "went for it." As I began to speak, the words went straight from my spirit to my tongue. God got His message across.

SUMMARY

- The Holy Spirit was promised, and given, just as Jesus said He would be.
- The promise of the Holy Spirit is the promise of His presence.
- We are to have an "overwhelming" experience with the Holy Spirit.
- The Holy Spirit is to teach us and remind us of the things/words of God.
- The Holy Spirit is to lead us.
- The Holy Spirit is to "bear witness" through us.
- The Holy Spirit pours out the Father's love on us.
- The Holy Spirit sets our minds on the things of the spirit.
- We are to keep in step with the leading of the Spirit.
- The Spirit affirms our relationship as children of our Father.
- The Spirit gives us hope.
- The Spirit works to make us holy and pure (sanctifies)
- The Spirit empowers us for living the life and ministry God calls us to.
- The Spirit brings us spiritual gifts and spiritual fruit.

Questions

1. Which of the activities of the Holy Spirit have you seen in your life? Which activities have you yet to see?
2. Do you and/or your church fellowship "eagerly desire spiritual gifts"?
3. Do you believe (and act out of that conviction) that you have supernatural power for every aspect of your life in God?

Chapter Seven

LIVING OUT OF OUR SPIRIT – I

The book of Galatians is the apostle Paul's strong argument for living by faith as opposed to living legalistically. In chapter one he is appalled that these groups of churches have been tempted, after receiving the good news of Jesus Christ, to go back to living by the Law. After reminding them of his own personal history with Jesus and the grace shown to him in chapters one and two, in chapters three and four he lays out 8 reasons why living by grace through faith is superior to living by the legalistic, rule-keeping. Then in chapters five and six, he answers the question, "If living by grace through faith is the superior way of life, how do you do that? What does this kind of living look like?"

<u>Gal. 5:5</u> For we through the Spirit, by faith, are waiting for the hope of righteousness. 6 For in Christ Jesus neither circumcision nor uncircumcision means anything, but faith working through love.

Living "Out Of" Faith

In living this kind of life, Paul makes the connection to the resources of the Holy Spirit. Literally, in the Greek language in which Paul wrote this book, he says, "For we through the Spirit, out *of faith*, are waiting...." Then he continues to point out that the thing they are arguing about — circumcision or uncircumcision, living by the law or not — isn't even the point. What is important is "faith working through love." So here in two verses Paul connects living by the Spirit with our faith, and then continues to make the point that faith must have an outlet. That is, faith must work itself out through love. Love is demonstrated faith; faith springs out of the Spirit/spirit.

Having Funerals

A few verses later, Paul continues,

16But I say, walk by the Spirit, and you will not carry out the desire of the flesh. 17 For the flesh sets its desire against the Spirit, and the Spirit against the flesh; for these are in opposition to one another, so that you may not do the things that you please. 18 But if you are led by the Spirit, you are not under the Law. 19 Now the deeds of the flesh are evident, which are: immorality, impurity, sensuality, 20 idolatry, sorcery, enmities, strife, jealousy, outbursts of anger, disputes, dissensions, factions, 21 envying, drunkenness, carousing, and things like these, of which I forewarn you, just as I have forewarned you, that those who practice such things will not inherit the kingdom of God. 22 But the fruit of the Spirit is love, joy, peace, patience, kindness, goodness, faithfulness, 23 gentleness, self-control; against such things there is no law. 24 Now those who belong to Christ Jesus have crucified the flesh with its passions and desires. 25 If we live by the Spirit, let us also walk by the Spirit.

Look at verse 24 again, "Now those who belong to Christ Jesus have crucified the flesh with its passions and desires." How do most Christians handle "the flesh with its passions and desires"? They try to discipline themselves. They try to bring the flesh under control. But what is Paul saying here? Pursue the Spirit. That's how you "fix" the flesh! Investing ourselves in pursuit of the Spirit, not in managing our sin, brings life. What are we focusing on? We don't fix the flesh by focusing on the flesh.

We don't live, however, in denial. If there are activities of the flesh operating in our lives, we deal with it. But we don't deal with it by discipline. Discipline comes about, yes. But discipline is a fruit (a product) of the Spirit (verse 23). In teaching this, one of the participants reminded us of how people are taught to snow ski. You are instructed to not look at your skis. You are instructed to look where you want to go. Thus it is with the spiritual life. Focus on where you want to go.

Notice again that this word says "have crucified the flesh...." Have crucified denotes past tense. Once I was talking with a brother in Christ who was sharing with me some "flesh" he was "struggling with." My advice to him was, "You know, you just need to have a funeral for that. Put it in the grave and be done with it. It's dead. You are dead to that from now on." Paul says this later in Galatians 6:

14 But may it never be that I would boast, except in the cross of our Lord Jesus Christ, through which the world has been crucified to me, and I to the world.

What is he saying? The world didn't have a hold on him anymore. The world could try to pull on Paul, but it didn't have any control over him anymore. Back to Galatians 5:24, he is saying that one who belongs to Christ Jesus can't be pulled by the flesh anymore. Consequently, with those whom the Lord has given me to "disciple" I encourage them, when tempted by something, to say (even out loud so they can hear themselves saying it), "That's not me anymore! I don't have to do that anymore." Before I knew Jesus, or had His life and resources within me, I gave in to those temptations. But now, that's not who I am anymore. It comes back to who I believe I am. Where does my identity come from? Knowing who I am gives me strength for what I do (or don't do). "That's not me anymore." Therefore that (temptation) doesn't have the pull on me anymore." And, once this response happens a few times, our enemy and his minions will give up on that temptation and try something else. Part of the activity of a spiritual life is to conduct a series of funerals.

Where's Our Focus?

In Galatians 5:16 Paul used the normal verb for walking ("walk by the Spirit"). But in verse 25 he uses a different verb. Let me re-re-re-emphasize that this verb was a military term. It meant to walk, rank and file, in formation. You, as a soldier, were to keep step with the person in front of you. You must put your left foot forward when he put his left foot forward, and put your right foot forward when he put his right foot forward. Keep in step. What was necessary was to keep your eyes on that person and to keep close enough that when that person turned or stopped you would also. See how that applies to our relationship with the Spirit of God? Again, if we are distracted and take our eyes off of Him, He may get to the corner and turn. We come along and say, "Where'd He go?" We are to keep "close" and keep our eyes on Him. We are to cultivate our ability to sense when and where He is leading us.

Galatians 6:7 Do not be deceived, God is not mocked; for whatever a man sows, this he will also reap. 8 For the one who sows to his own flesh will from the flesh reap corruption, but the one who sows to the Spirit will from the Spirit reap eternal life.

These verses lay out for us one of the dynamics of kingdom living. The kingdom of God operates on principles He has created — the way things work. One of the ways things work is "sowing and reaping." You don't throw apple seeds in the ground and expect to get cucumbers. What you put into the ground is what is produced later on. So, why would we go out and focus upon and invest our lives in things that bring death ...and expect that we will get by with it? To put it another way, the way I've told several people lately, what you feed grows. Are you feeding your flesh or are you feeding your spirit?

Remember what our spirits can do. We've looked at this earlier. We must keep remembering how our spirit has been created to function. As we remember these functions, it can cause expectations to rise up within me. I have been created for these purposes! I can (by the grace of God) do these things! If I know and believe that one of the purposes of my hand is to wrap itself around a small piece of wood with graphite on the end of it and write, then I will practice writing. If I know and believe that my spirit is made to function in certain ways, I will begin to practice those things.

Let's apply this to one of the functions of my spirit, namely, the exercise of spiritual gifts. Sometimes, people get a little crazy when they discuss spiritual gifts. For instance, people will ask me, "Do you speak in tongues?" "Yes." "Do you speak in tongues every day?" "Yes, I practice speaking in tongues." "Oh no! Practice? PRACTICE? Then it must not be a true spiritual gift!" But let's shift over to my experience of seminary. I went to a seminary, among other reasons, to hone and improve and "practice" the spiritual gift of teaching. Teachers can improve their teaching by teaching! So why look at, for instance, tongues and say that it is entirely spontaneous or ecstatic and yet not apply the same reasoning for teaching? If I believe that in this area (spiritual gifts) or other areas of the spiritual life I am CAPABLE of living in a certain way, it will help motivate me to pursue that area.

Becoming More Sensitive To Our Spirit

Remember my drawing of the three concentric circles? Many believers are aware of their bodies and aware of their soul. But their spirit is like a tiny dot deep inside them. How do we become more sensitive to and aware of our spirit?

Here are some of my suggestions:

1. Prayer: Ask

Tell God you want to live out of your spirit.

1 John 5: 14 This is the confidence which we have before Him, that, if we ask anything according to His will, He hears us. 15 And if we know that He hears us in whatever we ask, we know that we have the requests which we have asked from Him.

Of all of the prayers that we pray, this prayer is one which we may have confidence is "according to His will." God desires that we live out of our spirit. Therefore, we can pray this prayer with the confidence and expectation that He will answer us.

"Lord, I want to be a spiritual person. Do whatever You have to do in me to bring this about." Wanting to be a spiritual person, to live out of our spirit, is God's will. He hears us and will answer us. Prayer is meant to be a *dia-logue*, not a *mono-logue*. That means it's two-way: us to God and God to us. So ask...and then listen.

2. Cultivate Spiritual Senses

"Lord, heighten my spiritual senses." God has created us with five senses in the natural — sight, hearing, smell, taste, and touch. I believe He has given us corresponding spiritual senses — spiritual eyesight, spiritual hearing, spiritual smell, spiritual taste buds, and the ability to sense, spiritual, a touch from God.

Spiritual Sight

John 5:19 Therefore Jesus answered and was saying to them, "Truly, truly, I say to you, the Son can do nothing of Himself, unless it is something He sees the Father doing; for whatever the Father does, these things the Son also does in like manner. 20 "For the Father loves the Son, and shows Him all things that He Himself is doing; and the Father will show Him greater works than these, so that you will marvel."

Jesus didn't do anything except what He SAW the Father doing. Now, perhaps, he is talking about natural eyesight. I'm sure that Jesus was a very observant person. But, many times, Jesus saw what wasn't apparent to natural eyes (Luke 10:18; John 1:48). The way I put this into practice is this: most of the time wherever I go (restaurants, on the streets, at church meetings, home groups), I ask, "Father, show me what you are doing here." Then I just become alert and start "looking" for what He will show me. Jesus lived in both realms: the natural and the supernatural. I desire to live in, and "see" in both as well, with the supernatural, spiritual realm being the "more real."

Spiritual Hearing

John 10: 27 "My sheep hear My voice, and I know them, and they follow Me; 28 and I give eternal life to them, and they will never perish; and no one will snatch them out of My hand."

Jesus' sheep hear His voice. They hear His voice. His sheep have learned to recognize the voice of their Shepherd. They respond to His voice; they follow Him. "And I give eternal life to them...." Most of the time we hear "eternal life" our thoughts jump to heaven. What does Jesus say, in John 17:3, that "eternal life" is? It's knowing the Father and knowing the Son. Connecting this "definition" with John 10 we see that every time we follow His voice, we connect with and "know" the Father and the Son. Every time we hear Him and obey Him we experience eternal life. Don't immediately hear "eternal life" and think heaven. Yes, ultimately, eternal life is to be with and to know and experience the Lord forever and ever. But it starts now! This is part of what eternal life looks like.

<u>Is. 50:4</u> The Lord GOD has given Me the tongue of disciples,
That I may know how to sustain the weary one with a word.
He awakens Me morning by morning,
He awakens My ear to listen as a disciple.

Often, in the morning when I wake up, I will think about and pray this verse. It says that the Lord "awakens" not only me, but He awakens my ear to listen. This awakening is to listen **as a disciple**. What this says is that it should be my expectation, as I follow Jesus, as His disciple, to have the supernatural ability to hear Him every day.

As a disciple (remember the Jewish rabbinical system) the person came to a rabbi not only to learn what the rabbi knew, but to eat what the rabbi ate, to sleep where the rabbi slept, to relate to others the way the rabbi related to them, and to speak like the rabbi spoke. What Isaiah is saying is that he will awaken each day to hear what his Lord is saying and turn around and speak those words, and act toward others according to those words and, in doing so, will "sustain the weary one with a word." What a concept! What a promise!

A favorite statement of Jesus, as we read through the gospels, is "Whoever has ears to hear, let him hear." Jesus is talking about spiritual hearing, spiritual ears.

Spiritual Taste

Hebrews 6:4 For in the case of those who have once been enlightened and have tasted of the heavenly gift and have been made partakers of the Holy Spirit, 5 and have tasted the good word of God and the powers of the age to come, 6 and then have fallen away, it is impossible to renew them again to repentance, since they again crucify to themselves the Son of God and put Him to open shame.

The book of Hebrews is a letter of encouragement, of urging, to Jewish believers in Messiah Jesus. These believers were getting strong pressure from their families, friends, and Jewish leaders to revert to strict Judaism and abandon their faith in Jesus. The author of Hebrews is writing to point out the superiority of Christ and being His followers. "Don't go back! We have a greater covenant. We have a greater High Priest. We have a greater and lasting sacrifice. We have greater promises and hope."

The author, here in chapter 6, is either speaking about real people who have gone back to their former faith or he could be speaking hypothetically about what would be true if someone did revert. In either case, the author is saying that when following Jesus, a person "tastes" of both the heavenly gift and of the good word of God (v.5). Now, this could be speaking metaphorically, poetically.

But I know of people who are so spiritually sensitive in this area. They can walk into a room and get a taste in their mouths, sometimes "sweet" or sometimes "bitter" or rotten. When they have tasted something like sulphur, it is often an indication that there is demonic activity around. And this has proven true. This sounds very, very strange and weird to us. But have you ever read this book (Bible)??? There are so many "weird" occurrences in this book! We are so conditioned by our natural, scientific, rationally-minded (and limited) culture to believe many biblical reports aren't literally true. Please don't limit God. God is weird (the dictionary definition of "weird" is "what is outside of our experience").

I'm not saying we all will experience this same kind of "taste" all the time. But it is an example of how, potentially, our spiritual senses can be heightened and a way in which we can live out of our spirits.

<u>1Pet. 2:1</u> Therefore, putting aside all malice and all deceit and hypocrisy and envy and all slander, 2 like newborn babies, long for the pure milk of the word, so that by it you may grow in respect to salvation, 3 if you have tasted the kindness of the Lord.

Again, this may be a metaphorical "tasting" of the kindness of the Lord. But I've had experiences when I have sat and just enjoyed God's kindness. In some of those times I have, literally, had a wonderful taste in my mouth.

Spiritual Smell

<u>2Cor. 2:14</u> But thanks be to God, who always leads us in triumph in Christ, and manifests through us the sweet aroma of the knowledge of Him in every place. 15 For we are a fragrance of Christ to God among those who are being saved and among those who are perishing; 16 to the one an aroma from death to death, to the other an aroma from life to life. And who is adequate for these things?

This passage is one of Paul's natural pictures of spiritual truths. Paul pictures the "victory parade" of a Roman conqueror. The parade would consist of the victorious army marching through the city streets, followed by the victorious general, finally followed by the conquered people (usually walking in chains). The "parade" was preceded by and interspersed by people throwing sweet smelling garlands of flowers. To the conquerors, these smells spoke of victory, an aroma of "life to life." To the conquered, these smells spoke of "death to death."

The Lord says we smell. To some, we stink. To others, we smell like perfume. I have also smelled "in the spirit/Spirit." On a few occasions, during times when I was especially aware of God's presence, I have smelled roses. I have also walked into places and smelled what seemed like rotten garbage. In both cases there was no physical explanation of the smells. In those instances, and in so many other ways, our Lord "condescends" to give us these experiences, to direct us but also to just give us "kisses" of His kindness.

Spiritual Touch

There is touch and then there is **touch**. We see this in the story of the woman with the hemorrhage (Mark 5, Luke 8).

Jesus is walking among a crowd of people. The people are pressing in on Him and, I'm sure, bumping into and touching Him. Yet one woman forces her way through this throng and "touches" His garment. This touch stops our Lord dead in His tracks. What made the difference between their touch and hers? Her touch of faith made a withdrawal from His power. It was a spiritual touch.

In Acts 8 Philip (not the apostle Philip who stayed in Jerusalem) went up to Samaria, shared and demonstrated the kingdom, and revival breaks out and affects the whole city (would to our God that this would happen more and more now). Peter and John are sent from the Jerusalem church to check things out. As they are there they were "laying their hands on them and they were receiving the Spirit." How do we know that they were "receiving the Spirit"? The next verse says that Simon (the former sorcerer) "saw" something. "18 Now when Simon saw that the Spirit was bestowed through the laying on of the apostles' hands, he offered them money,....." Simon SAW something that occurred after a touch from the apostles. The apostles touched and the Spirit was released.

Ananias lays his hands on Paul and Paul's sight is restored. Paul reminds Timothy that he received a spiritual gift when the presbytery laid their hands on him (1 Tim. 4:14). This "laying on of hands" (for healing and/or for recognition of servant leadership, Acts 6:6) is one of the fundamentals of our faith according to the writer to the Hebrews (Hebrews 6:2).

Being supernatural beings, there can be a transfer from spiritual touch. Physical touch can also be healing to a person in certain circumstances (just as Jesus' physical touch to the leper was emotionally healing to him, no doubt, Mark 1:41).

All of the physical senses we have been given are "pictures", I believe of the spiritual senses we have been given. We can ask the Lord to heighten and develop these senses. I do this, in prayer, 2-3 times a week or when I am going to be with others in which there may be a ministry opportunity. "Lord, heighten my spiritual senses! I want to see and hear and smell and taste and touch what is in the spirit. I want to live in that realm more than I live in the natural realm."
Do we want a super-natural life? If we do, that means it is a life that is "super" (or "above") a natural life. If we are going to have a supernatural life, we are going to have supernatural experiences.

Having supernatural experiences is going to make us, many times, look "weird" or, as one of the ladies in this training said, "hokey." But we must come to the place of decision whether we want to risk looking "hokey" and live in, with, and by the spirit or live naturally and fit in. We don't' desire to look "weird" just for the sake of looking weird or calling attention to ourselves. But if we live by the Spirit, out of our spirit, it will be the true alternative lifestyle.

I believe — because I am talking to more and more Christians who are coming to believe there is more to the Christians life than they are experiencing — that living out of our spirit and by the life of the Holy Spirit within us is a growing hunger and desire of many, many believers. Many Christians have done all the "spiritual stuff" that has been recommended (Bible study, prayer, fasting, tithing/giving, etc.) but still find themselves empty. They find themselves powerless in the face of temptation. They find themselves impotent when they or someone dear to them gets sick. May we be stirred up in the spirit/Spirit! We will continue some practical suggestions in the next chapter.

SUMMARY

- Living "out of" our faith produces demonstrated life, notably, acts of love.
- It's spiritually productive to attend our own funeral!
- Focus on the things of the spirit and not on our flesh.
- Be more aware of our spiritual senses: sight, hearing, smell, taste, and touch.

Questions

1. What actions have you participated in recently that you could say sprang out of what you believe?
2. How much time have you spent focusing on building yourself up in the spirit?
3. Have you asked the Lord to heighten your spiritual senses?

Chapter Eight

LIVING OUT OF OUR SPIRIT - II

3. Live by (grow in) faith

<u>Hebrews 11:6</u> And without faith it is impossible to please Him, for he who comes to God must believe that He is and that He is a rewarder of those who seek Him.

It is impossible to please God without faith in our lives. It is impossible. Faith is the spiritual oxygen for our environment. Paul is even stronger: "Whatever is not of faith is sin" (Romans 14:23).

Faith is crucial for living. We are to live our whole life by faith. In another pictorial way, faith is the fuel for the engine of our spirit. Faith may be one of those "watermelon seed" concepts to us. We say the word, but it may be slippery to live it out. Nevertheless, faith must be demonstrated. We "believe" in principles; we "trust" a person. Faith is belief of a principle, a truth. But we must move from believing that truth to putting it into practice in any given situation through relying upon the Lord and seeing that truth acted out in our lives: "faith without works is dead" (James 2:26).

<u>Rom. 10:14</u> How then will they call on Him in whom they have not believed? How will they believe in Him whom they have not heard? And how will they hear without a preacher? 15 How will they preach unless they are sent? Just as it is written, "HOW BEAUTIFUL ARE THE FEET OF THOSE WHO BRING GOOD NEWS OF GOOD THINGS!" 16 However, they did not all heed the good news; for Isaiah says, "LORD, WHO HAS BELIEVED OUR REPORT?" 17 So faith comes from hearing, and hearing by the word of Christ.

Here is the progression:

Calling (upon the Lord) preceded by believing preceded by hearing preceded by preaching preceded by sending.

Yet, Paul says that it is possible that this progression produce no result. Why? Because, he says, there was no faith present in the hearers (this situation is affirmed in Hebrews, "for the word they heard did not profit them, because it was not united by faith in those who heard," 4:2).

But, here, faith comes by hearing and hearing by the "word" of Christ. Of the two words for "word" in the Greek language (logos and rhema), this is rhema. Although there is overlap in meaning in a few situations, basically "logos" means a body of truth. Jesus is called the Logos because He was the embodiment of the truth (John 1). Rhema, on the other hand, most often refers to truth applied to a specific situation. It may be a "word" directly spoken by God/Jesus/Holy Spirit. Or it may refer to the written word (logos) applied to a specific situation. Rhema is a "freshly spoken" truth. Rhema is a word for the moment. Rhema will never contradict the logos. Case in point: Jesus had told His disciples to go make disciples in all the nations (Matthew 28:18-20, a "logos" word). Philip, one of the seven (Acts 6) had gone to Samaria (Acts 8). So, perhaps Philip was thinking, "I need to go to the nations. I think I will go to Syria next." However, the Holy Spirit speaks to Philip (rhema word), "Go to the desert road." Philip heeds the rhema word and the Ethiopian eunuch is saved. Church tradition attributes to this African the discipling of his nation.

Faith comes by "hearing." This verse doesn't say that faith comes by having heard. Therefore, faith is an active, on-going process. It is to always be taking place. Every time we have a "hearing" — hear a "rhema", in that moment, we have the opportunity to exercise faith. I am not to have the option of hearing it and thinking about it for two weeks. In fact, if we do not act upon the promptings of faith we will either lose the opportunity, we will be thrown into disbelief, or this word will become mental assent only and not active faith.

<u>Ephesians 2:8</u> For by grace you have been saved through faith; and that not of yourselves, it is the gift of God; 9 not as a result of works, so that no one may boast.

A quick lesson in Greek grammar: in verse 8 is the word "that" ("that not of yourselves"). "That" is a relative pronoun. A relative pronoun corresponds to a noun in the sentence (or in the sentence or sentences preceding it). In the Greek language a relative pronoun must "agree" in case, number and gender with the noun it modifies. The Greek language has 3 genders: masculine, feminine, and neuter. So, the question is: what does "that" refer to? Does it refer to "grace" or to "faith"? Whatever "that" refers to, Paul tells us that it is a gift of God. "That" is of the neuter gender. So which, "grace" or "faith," is neuter? Neither one; both are feminine. What is the answer? Paul considers grace and faith to be a "package deal." Grace and faith are components of the saving work of God (the Greek word for "salvation" is neuter). Therefore, both grace and faith are gifts of God. We start our Christian life, having been given both grace and faith. Faith is a gift. We have it given to us.

Peter recognizes this in his second letter:

<u>2 Pet. 1:5</u> Now for this very reason also, applying all diligence, in your faith supply moral excellence, and in your moral excellence, knowledge, 6 and in your knowledge, self-control, and in your self-control, perseverance, and in your

perseverance, godliness, 7 and in your godliness, brotherly kindness, and in your brotherly kindness, love.

Notice Peter does NOT say to add faith. He says "in your faith" add these other qualities. Peter believes we start with faith. I cannot create any faith. But let me illustrate how I believe faith works. When a healthy baby is born that baby has muscles. They are small and tiny. But within those tiny muscle fibers, is the potential of large, well-functioning muscles. Faith is the same. We are "born" with faith fibers. They have potential to grow. We can cooperate with God in the growth process. We don't get more (quantity) muscles. We grow and strengthen the muscles we have been given. Faith needs to be nourished and exercised and it will grow. Many Christians ask God, "Lord, give me more faith." We don't need MORE faith. We need the faith we have to be STRONGER. I can imagine my Father, listening to my prayer for more faith, saying, "Son, come on. I've already given it to you."

This is why, when the disciples said, "Lord, increase our faith!" Jesus replied, "if you have the faith of a mustard seed...." (Luke 17:5-6). Jesus was revealing one of the ways the kingdom works. A mustard seed has the potential within it to explode and grow. The disciples were looking for a major release of faith. Jesus was affirming they had baby muscles but they could grow. Our faith has the potential to explode. We must begin to think that way. Many believers, as I myself did for years, focus on "not having enough faith." But a few years ago I started believing I DO have enough faith. I have within me the faith to do the impossible.

How am I nourishing these faith muscles? Recently, I wanted more breakthrough in the area of faith for physical healing. Therefore, since faith comes by hearing and hearing by the word of Christ, I carried around (on 3 X 5 cards) the words of Jesus about asking and receiving. I would pull them out several times a day and bathe myself in the truth of His words: I am exercising my faith muscles.

<u>Heb. 11:1</u> Now faith is the assurance of things hoped for, the conviction of things not seen.

Again, "hope" in Scripture is the absolute certainty that what God has promised He will fulfill. Hope is connected to the promises of God and to His faithfulness to perform them. Faith looks at the promises of God and says, "He promised them; they are going to happen!" Faith is also being certain of what we don't see. What faith does is to look at the unseen world and/or to the future of what God has promised and pulls it into the present world.

That is exactly what the Syro-Phoenician woman did (Matthew 15:21-28). She was making a nuisance of herself crying out to Jesus to heal her demonized daughter. The disciples wanted to send her away. Finally, Jesus said something that would have offending most Gentiles. He refers to her as a "dog." Jesus' point was to focus on His role of coming to the house of Israel. He didn't come, at this point, for the Gentiles (that was to come later, Acts 10, to Cornelius and then to Antioch and then to the Gentile world). But this woman's faith looked into the future, when Jesus' miraculous and powerful ministry would be for the Gentiles as well, and pulled that promise into her present world. Jesus was impressed. He commended her faith and performed healing for her daughter.

This is another reason we need to cultivate our spiritual eyesight, so that we can see the unseen. The negative dynamic operates the same way. Fear looks into the future and sees the worst happening. Fear is "negative faith" in operation. My wife calls fear "faith in hell." Fear goes down and grabs hold of what might happen and it literally causes an emotional reaction as if what we dread is already happening. Faith, on the other hand, believes that God is saving us. His salvific work is operating to bring us all of what He has promised. Hebrews 11:1 is now not only a definition of faith but also the operation of faith.

Then, according to the epistle by James, faith works (2:17-18, 26). Faith, if it is true faith, is evidenced. You can see faith being applied in living.

Faith can grow. Faith can become stronger. As I gave the earlier illustration of faith being a gift, is like muscles in a healthy baby. The muscle fibers are there. There exists within the DNA of that baby everything necessary for large, adult muscles. They just need the right ingredients to grow and become fully mature. When we are born spiritually, injected into our spirit is the DNA of faith with all the potential of fully grown, functioning "faith muscles."

How can faith grow?

- Read the Word of God and read the Word of God and read the Word of God until the Word is IN you!
- Rehearse what God has done (in your life, through your life).
- Read and listen to testimonies of others — what God has done for them.
- Relate to and "hang out" with people of great faith (this may be done personally — the best way — or through recordings, videos, books, etc.).
- Take opportunities to "walk out" your faith; be obedient to what God tells and shows you.

As an illustration of the exercise of faith, let's look at five scenarios in the life of Abraham.

ABRAHAM, OUR EXAMPLE OF FAITH

Romans 4:18 In hope against hope he believed, so that he might become a father of many nations according to that which had been spoken, "SO SHALL YOUR DESCENDANTS BE." 19 Without becoming weak in faith he contemplated his own body, now as good as dead since he was about a hundred years old, and the deadness of Sarah's womb; 20 yet, with respect to the promise of God, he did not waver in unbelief but grew strong in faith, giving glory to God, 21 and being fully assured that what God had promised, He was able also to perform.

Within a few verses, Abraham's life is condensed to show us his example of living by faith. Exercising his faith brought about the realization of what God had promised him. To begin, we see several things:

- There was nothing in the natural to see except what "spoke" *against* God's promise. In the natural, what God promised was impossible! Abraham's age, Sarah's age — all said, "No way!"
- Abraham didn't live in la-la land. He faced the facts (contemplated his own body). But he more than balanced these facts with God's promise.
- These verses say Abraham didn't become weak in faith (19) and "did not waver in unbelief" (20). But he did, didn't he? What about Ishmael? This is one of the wonders of God that I love. God, in reporting here about Abraham's life, looks at the whole of his life, the end or summary of his life here on earth, and declares Abe a man of faith! I take great comfort in this aspect of God's view of me!

(i.e., in 2 Peter 2:7, Lot—see his story in Genesis 19 — is called "righteous Lot"!!!!!)

Having this introduction, let's jump back into Abraham's story and see the progression of his faith.

- He heard.

    Gen. 12:1 Now the LORD said to Abram,
    " Go forth from your country,
    And from your relatives
    And from your father's house,
    To the land which I will show you;
    2 And I will make you a great nation,
    And I will bless you,
    And make your name great;
    And so you shall be a blessing;
    3 And I will bless those who bless you,
    And the one who curses you I will curse.
    And in you all the families of the earth will be blessed."

We have no indication at the end of Genesis 11 that Abraham was even seeking God. Yet, in these verses of chapter 12, God spoke to Abraham. We aren't told if this was an audible voice or if Abe heard these words in his mind. Nevertheless, God spoke to him and he heard. We've already seen this progression of hearing words from God in Romans 10:14-17. The Greek (Western world) mindset would say, "Faith comes by seeing." The Hebrew (and God's) mindset says, "Faith comes by hearing."

- He saw.

Gen. 15:5 And He took him outside and said, "Now look toward the heavens, and count the stars, if you are able to count them." And He said to him, " So shall your descendants be." 6 Then he believed in the LORD; and He reckoned it to him as righteousness.

When God begins to give us a promise, He desires to show us in many ways this is true. He may confirm His word to us in a number of ways. It may be a "picture" in the natural as He gave Abraham here. God shows Abe a visual object lesson of His promise = descendants. God may give us a vision or a dream to confirm His promise. But these confirmations are something we see. Abraham went from hearing to seeing.

- He meditated.

Rom. 4:20 yet, with respect to the promise of God, he did not waver in unbelief but grew strong in faith, giving glory to God, 21 and being fully assured that what God had promised, He was able also to perform.

Abraham thought. He meditated. He spent time filling his mind with God's ability to perform what He had promised. He spend time "giving glory to God," worshipping Him, focusing on the nature, character, and attributes of God. It was as if Abraham said, over and over, "God said this; God showed this. God said this; God showed me this. God said this; God showed me this." And, in this process, he became "fully assured" (the KJV and NIV say, "fully persuaded").

- He spoke.

Gen. 17:3 Abram fell on his face, and God talked with him, saying, 4 "As for Me, behold, My covenant is with you, and you will be the father of a multitude of nations. 5 "No longer shall your name be called Abram, but your name shall be Abraham; for I have made you the father of a multitude of nations.

From this encounter on, every time Abraham introduced himself, calling himself Abraham (meaning "father of a multitude"), he was speaking in faith. Every time he spoke his name, he spoke the promise. I'm sure that during some of those introductions, those hearing his name would look over his shoulder, looking for the "multitude" and think "you've got to be kidding me!"

I was at a Vineyard conference in the late 1980's. John Wimber was speaking. John began his sentence with, "God is getting ready to ..." Before John finished his sentence, I heard (in my mind) "Isaac." Then John finished his sentence "give you a new name." "Right now, God is giving people new names." I had my new name. Isaac ... it means "laughter." Although I haven't officially changed my name, I believe God was telling me this is one of the primary ways He sees me. Abraham and Sarah named their fulfilled promise, their son, laughter, because he brought them joy. If I see myself as Isaac, as one bringing joy to others, my identity shapes my activity.

- He acted.

Gen. 17:23 Then Abraham took Ishmael his son, and all the servants who were born in his house and all who were bought with his money, every male among the men of Abraham's household, and circumcised the flesh of their foreskin in the very same day, as God had said to him.

God had said that He was going to make Abraham the father of a multitude. God had promised that through Abraham a whole new nation would be created. God wanted a people who would be set apart unto Him. So, Abraham performed a physical act that said, "Yes, I believe that You, Lord, are doing this." Faith must lead to action.

I believe I am quoting Bill Johnson accurately when he says that faith, if not acted upon within 2 weeks, just becomes useless knowledge. We think we "know" - so that the next time the faith-truth is brought up, we respond with "Oh, I already know that" and do nothing about it. I don't know about the 2 weeks part, but I do know (from sad, personal experience) that this is the way it works! What I have been saying for years is that God gives us revelation for us to respond. Revelation isn't just for information; revelation demands a response.

- He received.

<u>Gen. 21:5</u> Now Abraham was one hundred years old when his son Isaac was born to him.

Now that the process was complete, as we saw condensed in Romans 4, Abraham's faith sees the beginning of the fulfillment of the promise. God gives a supernatural answer to what started verbally.

I believe we can learn about faith through Abraham. God wants to speak to us about His promises. They may come from the Scriptures. We may be reading a passage in the Bible which "leaps off" the page upon us and in us. It's a truth, a promise, which God wants us to take and run it through this process. He wants us to join our faith to His word and it will become true in our life (as opposed to the example of Israel given in Hebrews 4:2). He will encourage us along the way. He will send different kinds of confirmations. We can ask Him, "Lord, if this is your promise to me then give me something, something I can see, a vision, a dream." He wants us strong in faith. Faith is part of the fuel of the spirit.

4. Brokenness

"Many of God's servants are not able to do even the most elementary works. Ordinarily they should be enabled by the exercise of their spirit to know God's word, to discern the spiritual condition of another, to send forth God's messages under anointing and to receive God's revelations. Yet due to the distractions of the outward man, their spirit does not seem to function properly. It is basically because their outward man has never been dealt with. For this reason revival, zeal, pleading and activity are but a waste of time. As we shall see, there is just one basic dealing which can enable man to be useful before God: brokenness." (Watchman Nee, The Release of the Spirit)

God desires our "outer man" be broken. Nee uses two Scriptural examples of brokenness. One is in John 12 – "24 "Truly, truly, I say to you, unless a grain of wheat falls into the earth and dies, it remains alone; but if it dies, it bears much fruit. 25 " He who loves his life loses it, and he who hates his life in this world will keep it to life eternal." The outer husk of the wheat is our outer life, which needs to be broken in order to release what is inside, what is in our spirit. The other passage he mentions is the breaking of the alabaster vial, the costly perfume, to anoint Jesus (Mark

14). The connection I see is between the picture of Gideon's strategy against the Midianites with 2 Cor. 4:6-7. Gideon instructed his men to place their torches, their light inside clay firepots. Their only in-hand weapons for this warfare were trumpets in one hand and these firepots in the other. At the given signal the firepots were to be broken, revealing what? The fire within. In 2 Cor. 5 we are told that we have "the light of the knowledge of the glory of God in the face of Christ" and that this light (fire), this "treasure" is in a firepot, an earthen vessel. How does the fire, the light, get out? By the breaking of ourselves, everything that is not of the spirit/Spirit.

I believe that everything God brings our way in life is either to strengthen the inner man or to break the outer man. He wants to do away with anything that we may be relying upon other than Him. Recently, the young man who (with my wife) ministers at a lower socio-economic apartment complex to kids was seeing more chaos than in the two years they had been there. He tried a number of "strategies" to stop the chaos in the children's lives and in their relationships. Nothing was working. On the way home one evening he was complaining to the Lord. The Lord, essentially, told him that the problem was he was relying upon himself and not the Lord. When he "shifted" his faith, his reliance to the Lord, the environment shifted and peace came. I have witnessed this dynamic so many times in my own life as well. Have you?

So, my suggestions for becoming more sensitive to your spirit are: (1) ask for it; (2) cultivate your spiritual senses; (3) grow in faith; and (4) willingly be broken.

Practical Considerations For Walking In The Spirit

1. Get quiet

<u>Psa. 4:4</u> Tremble, and do not sin; Meditate in your heart upon your bed, and be still. Selah.

<u>Mark 1:35</u> In the early morning, while it was still dark, Jesus got up, left the house, and went away to a secluded place, and was praying there.

<u>Psalm 131:2</u> Surely I have composed and quieted my soul; Like a weaned child rests against his mother, My soul is like a weaned child within me.

We live in a busy, busy world. We live in a loud world. It is difficult, and requires intentionality, to get alone, to get quiet, and to listen to God. Many times we aren't aware of what is going on in our spirit because of all the noise. Do whatever it takes to get alone. Perhaps you have a special place you can go to regularly. Do it. Make it a priority.

It's also important to get quiet internally. When we try to get quiet a million thoughts crowd into our brains. I have found a couple of things help me. First, I pray that the Lord Himself will surround my mind and not let anything in He wouldn't want there. I ask Him to place a "hedge" around my mind. Second, I keep a pad of paper nearby so that if any stray "I gotta do this" thought arises I can quickly jot it down and get it off my mind. Third, I just focus (I mean concentrated focus) on Him. Just Him. Remind yourself to Whom you are presenting yourself. Quiet your soul. Listen.

2. Command your soul

<u>Judges 5:21</u> "The torrent of Kishon swept them away,
The ancient torrent, the torrent Kishon.
O my soul, march on with strength.

<u>Psa. 42:5</u> Why are you in despair, O my soul?
And why have you become disturbed within me?
Hope in God, for I shall again praise Him
For the help of His presence.

11 Why are you in despair, O my soul?
And why have you become disturbed within me?
Hope in God, for I shall yet praise Him,
The help of my countenance and my God.
Psa. 103:1 Bless the LORD, O my soul,
And all that is within me, bless His holy name.
2 Bless the LORD, O my soul,
And forget none of His benefits;

Ps. 116:7 Return to your rest, O my soul,
For the LORD has dealt bountifully with you.

Psa. 62:5 My soul, wait in silence for God only,
  For my hope is from Him.

Psa. 146:1 Praise the LORD!
Praise the LORD, O my soul!

Deborah, Barak, David and other psalmists commanded their soul. It is as if their spirit comes out of them, walks and turns around, faces the soul, and starts barking orders: "March", "Hope in God", "Bless the Lord", "Forget none of His benefits", "Return to your rest"(or, in other words, "Stop being anxious. Stop it!"), "Wait in silence for God only", and

"Praise the Lord!" This person is talking to himself/herself ... and it's OK!

This is giving our spirit the freedom to be in control, to control and order our soul around. Many of us, I fear, live life passively in subjection to our souls. We are carried away by our thoughts, our emotions, and choices we make. We feel helpless against them or that this is just the way people live. No! We can command our soul to "get in line" with God's program, with His way of living. We must remember that this is an exercise in futility (or craziness) unless His Spirit living in our spirit, enables us. I am being strengthened with power in my inner man by His Holy Spirit. My fellow believers, you have more power than you think you do. You have more authority than you believe that you do. Again, one of the great strategies of our enemy Satan is to get us to believe that we are powerless.

I must command my soul to "wait in silence for God only." I must because I am so very often pulled to not to wait but act, not to trust in God only but in something or someone else. I am to trust in Him alone. If I were to lean on a chair to the point that if you pulled it out from under me I would fall, then I am "trusting" in that chair. It alone holds me up. Again, we believe in principles or truths, but we trust a person. That is a spiritual exercise—to trust in the Lord Himself.

Praising the Lord is sometimes a sacrifice (Heb. 13:15). Sometimes we just don't FEEL like praising Him. Our emotions are in control. Or, our thoughts might be saying, "God didn't come through for me this week. I don't want to praise Him!" Our mind is in control. Many times what prevents us from praising is pride and/or self-pity. I don't want to praise the Lord. But we can bring forth praise when our spirit is in control. So we praise Him and we praise Him and we keep praising Him and soon our soul (and even our body) catches up with our spirit!

3. Begin to interact with God

I say "interact with God" rather than "pray." Praying is often thought of as talking to God. But that's just ½ of prayer, as I've mentioned before. If I get up in the morning and say, "Good Morning!" to my wife and talk awhile and go to work or an appointment, then come home in the evening and talk to her but ... never listen ... has real communication taken place? Yet we do that with God all the time. "Dear God... (talk, talk, talk, talk, talk) ... Amen." We never listen. Perhaps we should. Perhaps He wants to respond to all of our talking. Again, I point out, prayer is a dialogue. When I talk to God I EXPECT Him to talk back to me (He "talks" in a variety of ways). Col. 4:2 says, "Devote yourselves to prayer."

4. Go in faith

I've already written quite a bit about faith. But believe that you can live out of your spirit. Believe that Father desires this for you. I (we) must get ruthless with unbelief. I "go for the jugular" on thoughts of doubt and unbelief if they attempt to crowd in. I am going to keep myself in faith, in the truth. If I detect unbelief I ask the Lord, "Lord, why do I still have unbelief?" I may attack unbelief by going to the Scriptures and reading a portion that present the truth I'm contending for. I will read it over and over and over and over and over. I will read it until it get off the pages of my Bible and gets into my spirit. I cannot afford to live in unbelief (if I'm aware of it. And if I'm not aware, I can trust the Holy Spirit to point it out to me.). "Without faith it is impossible to please Him" (Heb. 11:6).

5. Persist

Keep doing it! Keep doing it! "Ask (and keep on asking) and it will be given to you; seek (and keep on seeking) and you will find; knock (and keep on knocking) and it will be opened to you" (Matt. 7:7). "You will seek Me and find Me when you search for Me with all your heart" (Jer. 29:13). God wants to be found. He wants to speak. He wants us to live out of our spirit. So, we must keep going back and keep going back and keep going back. We must persist.

6. Wait and Listen

Don't talk all the time. Madam Guyon, a passionate believer in the 1600's, had a "scandalous" love affair with the Lord. She was imprisoned for years for writing a torrid commentary on the Song of Songs. She made people feel uncomfortable by the way she talked of her love for the Lord. She said that during her personal times with the Lord she would sit and get still. Then, after a while, she would just quietly utter His name: "Jesus ... Jesus ... Jesus." He comes when we call Him!

7. Journal

This is helpful if you find it helpful. I have kept a journal for decades. I write my prayers, God's responses and words to me, the work Father is doing in my life, the work I desire Him to do in my life. I write some of the prophetic words given to me, the dreams and visions I have. Every couple of years, I will take the journals and re-read them and highlight those places that I believe God has spoken to me. This way I can quickly go through them and pick up these conversations. Then I can apply faith to these words and be encouraged by them.

8. Respond

In some form or fashion, respond to what the Lord is showing you or doing in your life. Every revelation demands a response. Our Father doesn't give us these words and experiences to just add them to our intellectual data files. Remember, this is a relationship. He expects us to respond.

Our response may be worship; it may be repentance; it may be taking action in some form (feed the poor, pray for the sick, go ask forgiveness of a brother or sister). If you come out of a time with the Lord and feel that He is asking you to do something ... DO IT! Do it as soon as possible. Time delays cause hearts to wane, convictions to melt.

Years ago, while I was in this process, meeting with the Father, He brought to my mind an incident that happened when I was in college, before I was a Christian. The university football team was going to play in the Orange Bowl that year. Tickets to the game were on sale at a reduced price to students. My friend and I bought a number of tickets, telling the ticket office we were scheduling a bus trip to the game. We "scalped" the tickets, charging much more than what we paid. We were pretty proud of ourselves for making the money. Well, even though I knew I was forgiven of this sin, Father was bringing it up because I had never made restitution for it and He was asking me to now. So, I traveled the 3 ½ car trip to the university. I was able to see the ticket manager (the same man who was ticket manager when I was in college) and I told him the whole story. I told him I was there to pay for the tickets or receive any other consequence. He was stunned. He said that they knew that this kind of scalping had occurred all the time. He said that this was the first time anyone had ever come in and admitted being a part. He just thanked me and told me I could go. My point was that coming out of my time with the Lord I felt that He wanted me to take care of this, to DO something. So I obeyed as fast as I could.

9. Enter into the process often

I wouldn't say that everyone needs to have a "daily quiet time." That can become legalistic and without life. But I believe and have seen that the more often we enter into this process of cultivating our relationship with Father and living out of our spirit, the more we will WANT to be involved in this process and in His presence. It is said that John Wesley noted that on the days he was especially busy he would rise even earlier so that he could spend more time with the Lord at the start of the day.

10. Watch your motives

I have realized, from time to time, that I would go to the Lord to "get stuff." I would get into a habit that every time I would come to Him I was asking for something, instead of coming just to be with Him, to hear from Him.

11. Get up every day expecting to be spiritual

Expect that day that you will have spiritual experiences, that God will show you things in the supernatural, that He will have you participate in what He is doing on the earth. You (and I) have a Father Who wants you to be successful at living out of your spirit!

12. Immerse yourself in the things of the Spirit

Galatians 6:7 Do not be deceived, God is not mocked; for whatever a man sows, this he will also reap. 8 For the one who sows to his own flesh will from the flesh reap corruption, but the one who sows to the Spirit will from the Spirit reap eternal life.

Sow to the Spirit. How do we do that? One of the ways I "sow to the Spirit" is to read or listen to people who live out of their spirit. I am encouraged by those who are examples of the kind of person I want to be. There are a lot of good books written by wonderful, believing authors. But I usually will ask the Lord if I'm supposed to read a particular book. There are several books, written by these spiritual role models, that I will go back to every few years and re-read them. There are certain writings that, when I read them, I feel my fires getting stoked.

A second way of sowing to the Spirit is by hanging out with people who do. If we aren't seeing much "spiritual" or "supernatural" happenings, perhaps it is because we aren't placing ourselves in position to experience them. Perhaps we are spending most of our time with people who do not share our desire to grow in the supernatural and spiritual nature of the kingdom of God.

A third way of sowing to the Spirit is by just putting yourself at risk. John Wimber used to say, "Faith is spelled R-I-S-K." It's true. We can be sensing something is going on in our spirit or in the environment in which God has us and be reluctant or do nothing about it. Fear...of embarrassment, of ridicule, of failure, of a multitude of things...can limit or shut down spiritual activity. When I risk stepping out into the spiritual, my faith grows. The more I see and participate in, the more I will expect. What if you risk and step out to give a word or pray a prayer or do something you feel the Lord is saying and you "strike out"? Then, learn! Learn from the experience. Just say, "Lord, I know I'm in training. Teach me. What happened? I want to improve next time."

13. Demonstrate Acts of Love

<u>Gal. 5:6</u> For in Christ Jesus neither circumcision nor uncircumcision means anything, but faith working through love.

Our faith really doesn't mean anything unless it is "evidenced" or shown. If we live out of our spirit, controlled by the Spirit of a God Who is love (1 John 4:8), then we will be loving. My friend and a recent mentor, Bob Mumford (author of The Agape Road, Lifechangers Library, 2006), defines biblical love (Greek word agape) as "I have a desire to do you good; that desire is not mine; it comes from the Father; I am now looking for occasion to do you good. If agape is really present, it has to manifest."

A spiritual person is a person who does not withdraw from their world but impacts it with the love of God.

I want to live out of my spirit. I want to live among a people who live out of their spirits. I want to exhort, urge, and encourage believers everywhere to live out of their spirit. What would it look like if a whole community of faith were living this way? How would the kingdom of God advance in an area where sons and daughters of the Father were tapping into this immense resource?

I want to cultivate a lifestyle that is so totally dependent upon the Lord and upon His Spirit living in my spirit. Not only will this be nourishing and refreshing to me but it will be contagious. This kind of living is attractive. It is the kind of living you can live. This is my prayer for you:

<u>Philem. 25</u> The grace of the Lord Jesus Christ be with your spirit.

SUMMARY

- Faith is a gift which we receive when we trust in Jesus.
- Faith can grow just like a muscle.
- Abraham's faith journey: he heard; he saw; he meditated; he spoke; he acted; then he received.
- Everything God brings into our lives is to either strengthen the inner man or break the outer man.

Questions

1. When, in your life, can you say you have "lived by faith"?
2. Where is your quiet place?
3. Have you ever commanded your soul? If so, has it "worked"?
4. Have you ever considered that prayer is a two-way conversation?
5. What do you think of my statement: "Every revelation demands a response"? What responses have you made to the revelation God has given you?

AN AFTERWORD

Often, when people read a book or hear a speaker, they get the idea that the author/speaker is an expert in the arena in which they have made the presentation. By no means do I present myself as an "expert" in living out of my spirit. I, like you, am doing my best to depend upon God to take me further in seeing this work out in my life. I don't see daily or weekly progress. But, as I look back over the years of my life, I am encouraged to see a greater "connectivity" with the Spirit of God in my spirit. I am spurred on by Micah 7:8 — "Do not rejoice over me, O my enemy. Though I fall I will rise; though I dwell in darkness, the LORD is a light for me." Jack Taylor, my spiritual father and mentor, is 80 years old. He has walked with God and been in ministry since being a teenager. When people have asked him how he has "made it", how he has been consistent in his walk and growth in the Lord, Jack replies, "I've just gotten up one more time than I've fallen down!" That's what I'm trying to do. That's what I'm encouraging you do it. Be encouraged; be persistent; fight the good fight (it IS a fight!); finish the race. Blessings!